Highland Drove

Also by John Keay

INTO INDIA
A Short Introduction to India and its Peoples

WHEN MEN AND MOUNTAINS MEET
The Explorers of the Western Himalayas 1820–75

THE GILGIT GAME
The Explorers of the Western Himalayas 1865–95

INDIA DISCOVERED
The Achievement of the British Raj
(Windward Books)

ECCENTRIC TRAVELLERS
(published jointly with BBC Publications)

JOHN KEAY

Highland
Drove

JOHN MURRAY

© John Keay 1984

First published 1984
by John Murray (Publishers) Ltd
50 Albemarle Street, London WIX 4BD

Typeset by Inforum Ltd, Portsmouth
Printed and bound in Great Britain
by The Pitman Press, Bath

British Library Cataloguing in Publication Data
Keay, John
Highland drove.
1. Cattle trails—Scotland—Highlands
2. Herders—Scotland—Highlands
I. Title
636.2'083   SF196.G7
ISBN 0–7195–4105–0

FOR THE DROVERS
Julia Keay, Russell Buchanan, Gavin Douglas,
George Knight, Jean-Pierre de Rohan, Chris Wiper

Contents

Illustrations

ACKNOWLEDGEMENTS

Nos 1, 5 and 6, Photo: Blair Urquhart; no 2, by courtesy of the
Victoria and Albert Museum; nos 3, 10, 11, 12 and 14, Photo:
Jean-Pierre de Rohan; no 4, by courtesy of the National Museum
of Antiquities, Scotland; nos 7, 8, 9 and 13, Photo: Alan
Thomson; no 15, Photo: James Mitchell; no 16, Photo: Russell
Buchanon; Sketch-map, Denys Baker

Acknowledgements

To list all those who have in some way contributed to this book and to the drove it describes would leave precious little room for the text. Cattle droving always depended on the goodwill of thousands and so does the book. My thanks, then, to everyone, whether or not they are included by name.

For original material and recollections of the droving trade I am indebted to the late Hugh MacGillivray of Dunbeg, Ian MacGillivray of Oban, Alex MacDougal of Tarbert, Lachlan Fletcher of Arnisdale, Eoghann MacLachlainn of South Uist, Lachie MacKinnon of Elgol, Donald Cameron of Fort William, and Sir Donald Cameron of Lochiel. James Crerar of Dalmally translated *The Song of the Drover* and Tim Williams of Duror found the John Clare verses. Many others have written to me of their family connections with droving and of local droving associations. In particular I must thank John Skinner of Inverfearn, D. and L. Christie of Perth, Mrs Agnes Calder of Perth, Mrs M. Dawson of Fochabers, Mrs J. Menzies of Perth, and Thomas Reid 'cattle dealer, retd'. The Scottish Arts Council were the first to support the idea of a book on droving and I am grateful for their patience over the years it has taken to come to fruition.

The drove itself was financed by a contribution from the Highlands and Islands Development Board and by the overall sponsorship of Matthew Gloag and Son, manufacturers of Famous Grouse Whisky. Alan Scott at the HIDB and, at Gloag's, Matthew Gloag, Tricia Lang and Martin Banks in effect made it possible. Additionally Scottish Agricultural Industries (Arthur Phillips) provided all the feedstuffs, Land Rover (Tom O'Connor) provided a vehicle, and Janet Buchanan of Portsonachan provided the ponies. The value of their contributions should be obvious from the text. Further sponsorship in kind was offered by Edward MacBean and Co. Ltd, Berghaus Ltd, Thermawear (Damart) Ltd and Blacks of Greenock. Chris Smart provided Jody, the most capable of cattle dogs, and Judy Bowser of Killin, Alison Craig of Appin, and Chris Robb of Kilchrennan, helped to outfit the ponies.

The cattle were eventually found with the assistance of the Highland Cattle Society, Hugh MacDonald of Oban, David Fellowes of

Dalmally, Michael Gibson of Dallas, and Sandy Gordon of Lude. Their sale was masterminded by James Weir, United Auctions, and Capt. Ben Coutts.

Hugh MacDonald and Capt. Coutts also belong in that select group of people whose hospitality and encouragement added an extra dimension to the drove. Others whose kindness excelled all reasonable definitions of courtesy were Mr and Mrs Wakefield of Glen Drynoch, Ian MacKinnon, John MacKinnon and Robert Kelly of Strathaird, Ian Campbell of Broadford, Terry Nutkins of Kylerhea, Sandy Ferguson of Greenfield, Hamish Menzies and Alasdair MacDonald of Black Mount, Mr and Mrs Bob Bisset of Invermeran, Mr and Mrs Jim Stretch of Meggernie, and Mr and Mrs Peter Halley of Crieff.

Besides those already mentioned permission was received from the following to cross their ground and in some cases to make a night stance on it: Department of Agriculture and Fisheries for Scotland (Mr A. Henry, Portree, and Mr C. G. Davidson, Inverness); The Forestry Commission (Scotland); D. J. Morrison, Carbost; MacLeod Estates and Gideon Macrae, Glenbrittle; Ian Campbell, Sconser; Ian Anderson, Strathaird; John Anderson, Torrin; George Campbell, Broadford Hotel; Ian Noble, Eilean Iarmain; W. Finlayson, A. McHattie, J. Clark and D. Murray, Broadford; G. Oliphant, Kylerhea; Major James Ellice, Glenelg; D. MacKenzie, E. Cameron and A. MacLean, also Glenelg; The Hon. G. M. H. Wills, Eilean Reach; J. MacBeath, Balvraid; Julian Richmond-Watson, Arnisdale; Capt. H. Birkbeck, Kinlochourn; Major W. G. Gordon, Glen Quoich; the Lord Burton, Dochfour; H. S. MacAdam, Pitlochry; Sir Donald Cameron of Lochiel, Achnacarry; Mr and Mrs Campbell, Corriechoillie; John Sutherland, Wick; British Aluminium Co. Ltd, Fort William; Miss Maxwell MacDonald, Corrour; Robin Fleming, Black Mount; Mrs Smith, Achallader; Economic Forestry Group Limited, Moffat (D. Newton) and Crieff (D. E. Carter); R. Stroyan, Boreland; Mrs Sands, Morenish; Mr Morris, Kinnell; North of Scotland Hydro-Electric Board, Tummel Bridge; Messrs Taylor Bros, Ardeonaig; J. F. Priestley, Invergeldie.

For their determined efforts to seek out all these landowners and tenants I am greatly indebted to officials of the DAFS in Oban, Inverness and Portree, and to the Scottish Landowners Federation, especially Lindsay Anderson, Inverness, and T. S. Drew, Perth. Messrs MacGrigor Donald and Co. and the Scottish Rights of Way Society offered legal guidance, and the Northern and Tayside Constabularies, the Ministry of Defence, and the Society for the Prevention of Cruelty to Animals gave specialised advice and assistance.

Others provided encouragement which it is less easy to categorise. With Graham Noble, once of Glenelg, the idea of actually recreating a drove was first nurtured; he helped with the preliminary research and it was sad that he could not come along. Hugh MacGregor of Thornhill lent experience gained riding ponies along a similar route, Hamish MacInnes of Glen Coe offered advice on conditions around Rannoch Moor, J. P. S. Hunter of Fort William identified some of the problems, Jim Mallows of Kilmelford supplied the foot-bath and, in Crieff, the Arduthie Hotel; Hugo Strathearn and Major Jock Stewart of Ardvorlich provided a warm welcome. Murdo MacKenzie of the *MV Glenmallie* also went out of his way to be helpful.

That leaves just the drovers. At different times on the drove Luke Casey and David Hannington of the BBC, Tricia Lang and Martin Banks of Famous Grouse, numerous representatives of the SPCA, Arthur Phillips, Irvine Butterfield, Richard Wood, Bill MacLutchie, Donald Bain, Tim and Ony Williams, Christina Noble and many others joined the drove, walked along with us and enlivened the routine. My thanks to all for their help and for their company.

To Julia, George, JP, Gavin, Russell and Chris thanks would be an impertinence. The dedication of this book is the nearest I can get to an acknowledgement that it is their work more than mine.

'They'll just lie down and die'

Ideas are harmless. Only when they become obsessions does one have to bestir oneself.

Five years ago, wading through the bracken and then scrambling up steep heathery slopes, I climbed above the Ferry Inn at Glenelg in Wester Ross. It was high summer. The bracken gave off its bitter woody smell and on the shelves of rock near the top the lichen was caked and crumbly. An invisible lark trilled on the breeze. The day was one for drowsy speculation. Ignoring the hazy outline of the Cuillin mountains, I chose a boulder near the edge of the void which here separates the Scottish mainland from the Isle of Skye. The void is a canyon, deep and apparently land-locked; it came as a rude surprise when a warship slipped silently through the strait, its radar scanning the cliffs and its bridge towering above the Inn. At its narrowest point the strait, or kyle, is about six hundred yards wide; from my vantage point to a spot at the same height on the opposite side must have been over half a mile. But it looked as if you could lob a stone across. In pre-Christian days giants like Finn MacCoul passed over this gap in a single stride – just as the pylons do today.

Down below, the little ferry chugged back and forth, four cars at a time. To stem the ferocious current it zigged and zagged with wondrous precision, a bow wave leaping unexpectedly on one tack and then disappearing on the next. Mysterious eddies bellied and swirled just off the rocks which lined each side of the channel. Here the whiskered nose of a seal breaks the surface and otters wind their amphibious way through black, slapping waters. From up on top you would need binoculars to see them. But anything as big and hairy and horned as a Highland cow would be plain enough.

Two hundred years ago this stretch of treacherous water was the annual arena for one of the most remarkable sights in the British Isles. In autumn, when the grass had lost its colour and the bracken was just beginning to turn, a river of cattle with men and dogs and ponies came pouring down the glen on the Skye side. The stream of beasts flowed ceaselessly for two or three weeks and at intervals during that time, when the tide was just right and the wind favourable, rowing boats massed just off the rocks and amidst scenes of frantic activity the cattle were driven into the water and escorted out into the channel. They crossed in their thousands, like a migration of lemmings, the water becoming prickly with horns. Oarsmen cursed, drovers shouted, dogs barked, cattle bellowed and, if all went well, after twenty minutes of frantic paddling, the leading beasts would scrabble on the cobble stones of the Glenelg slipway and climb, streaming with water, onto the Scottish mainland.

Sometimes a beast was lost, swept away on the tidal current, sometimes a boat upturned. But day after day the migration continued. On either side men swarmed between the inns and the water's edge. Their cattle filled the level ground and were stacked up the hillsides. From a hundred rough shelters of dry stone and turf the smoke of peat fires billowed across the scene. You can still see the outline of these shelters, now just a ring of stones partly hollowed into the hillside. The men and the cattle come no more; even the ferry is threatened with closure. Soon the otters and the seals will have the place to themselves.

Many of the beasts that took part in this annual migration had been bred on Skye. From Sleat and Strath, Bracadale, Snizort and Kilmuir they had been herded from the hill pastures to the Skye markets. 'I saw the picturesque troop go past,' wrote a contemporary, 'wildly beautiful brutes of all colours – black, red, cream-coloured, dun and tan; all of a height too and so finely bred you could hardly distinguish the one from the other.' At the makeshift markets they changed hands and were formed into droves of anything from twenty-five head to two hundred and fifty. Thence they took the road through Broadford to the kyle. Along the way they interleaved with other droves from further afield. Cattle from the Outer Hebrides – Lewis, Harris, the Uists and Benbecula – had usually been ferried across the Minch in open boats and landed at various points along the west coast of Skye. Others had been swum or ferried from Skye's satellite islands – Raasay, Scalpay, Soay. As they wound round the Cuillins at the island's narrow waist the procession of beasts, men, dogs and ponies became an unbroken stream surging towards the kyle, the first great bottle-neck on the journey to the Lowlands.

On a trek of perhaps two hundred miles in all, this crossing to Glenelg was only one of many perils. The most difficult terrain still lay ahead. There were high passes at which the island cattle would baulk and peat bogs as treacherous as quicksands; swollen rivers could be more dangerous than the open sea; and the longer the going the greater the risk of the cattle deteriorating.

But somehow the whole mystique and challenge of Highland droving only came home as I peered down into the strait at Glenelg. That vision of how it used to be, glimpsed during a drowsy afternoon on the cliff tops, lodged in my mind. A hundred, maybe two hundred, beasts at a time bobbing about in that malevolent channel – how on earth was it done? How did they tackle the bogs, the rivers and the rocky passes? And how did they manage to keep the cattle in good condition? There was only one way to find out. The fanciful notion of actually trying to restage a drove suddenly became a pressing imperative. No longer an idea, it was an obsession.

Living in the Highlands, loving them yet resigned neither to the perversity of their climate nor to the tragedy of their history, I saw the droving trade and the idea of recreating a drove as a way of coming to terms with the place. It was more than just a question of 'take walk, make book' – the White Man's supposed purpose in life as construed by a perceptive and over-explored African chief. I wanted to experience and participate in the life of an area which had been my home for a decade but not my birthright. How better than by crossing the hills with cattle and thus participating in a commercial activity which, during nearly two hundred years, had been the economic life-blood of the region?

For cattle were to the Highlands as fish to the Faeroes or furs to the Eskimos. They were the area's one exportable commodity; breeding, rearing and selling beef cattle became a national preoccupation. Before the late nineteenth century the complete absence of transport meant that the flow of this trade depended entirely on the skills of those anonymous heroes, the Highland drovers. Each year these rugged and wily characters reappeared in the furthest glens and islands. Often they took the beasts on trust giving just a small deposit plus a promissory note redeemable when they had successfully resold the cattle at one of the Lowland markets. Then they formed up their drove, marshalled their dogs and their herdsmen and, bestriding a little pony, set off across some of the most romantic but inhospitable scenery in Europe.

> What preparations were made for these gatherings on which the rent and income of the year depended! What a collecting of cattle, of drovers and of dogs – the latter being the most interested and excited of all the members of the caravan. What speculation as to how the market would turn out. What a shaking of hands in boats and wayside inns by the men in homespun cloth, gay tartans, or in the more correct new garbs of Glasgow or Edinburgh tailors! What a pouring in from all the glens, increasing at every ferry and village, and flowing on, a river . . . of great and small, to the market!

The Reverend Norman MacLeod, chaplain to Queen Victoria and 'one of the most notable ecclesiastics that Scotland has ever produced', captured the colourful side of droving. There was something intensely exciting about the idea of all those men and beasts pouring in from every corner of the Highlands; the trickle becoming a stream, a river, a flood; and the shaking of hands and the drinking of drams rising towards the crescendo of the great market, the tryst. In the eighteenth century the usual destination of this flood was the little town of Crieff in Perthshire. At the foot of the hills and abreast the Highland Line (that imaginary frontier between the Grampian mountains and the more level Lowlands), Crieff was a natural market at the gateway between two worlds. For the drovers, whether they came from Caithness and Cromarty in the far north or from Argyll and Islay in the south-west, it was a convenient crossroads. For the buyers, Scottish or English, it was simply the last outpost of civilisation to which they were willing to venture. The tryst was thus both a Highland and a national occasion and a suitably social climax for the drovers.

Today, to a limited extent and that thanks largely to subsidies, the cattle trade does still survive. In September, as the last of the mobile holiday homes heads south, lorries converted into cattle trucks by the addition of a 'float' or superstructure lumber onto Highland roads. On market days they grind up and down the glens in ponderous convoys heading for Stirling, Lanark and England. But each year there are less; sheep have long since ousted cattle as the mainstay of Highland agriculture and sheep are now themselves making way for conifers. The spectacle bears no comparison with the great surge of shaggy beasts which once poured through the passes. It lacks the finesse, it lacks the significance and it lacks the glamour.

If most of the cattle are gone so are most of the people and most of their way of life. Without the conviviality of being part of a massive communal event any latterday attempt to restage a drove could not be remotely authentic. It would be necessary to compromise at every stage. I accepted that and, as I watched the ferry swinging on the current in the kyle at Glenelg, I thought that here might well be a case in point. But even then, even with compromises and concessions, was it actually possible?

Of all the drove routes that converged on Crieff much the most challenging and romantic, and probably one of the busiest, was this route from Skye and the Outer Hebrides. After the Cuillin mountains and the crossing to the mainland most of the droves headed south over the switchback hills to Glen Garry and thence down to the Great Glen. At Spean Bridge, the second major bottle-neck on the route, the droves divided, some going east, others west, to work round the massif of Ben Nevis; both routes involved hard climbing. They rejoined at the top of Glen Coe for the long and treacherous slog across Rannoch Moor. Then came a choice of Glen Lyon or Glen Dochart with Loch Tay and Strathearn to follow.

No route could offer more in the way of natural splendour nor better evoke those maudlin memories which make up so much of Highland history. Additionally – and this was the deciding factor – the West Highlands have fewer roads, towns and enclosed fields, and more wide open spaces, than anywhere else in the country. In this respect the dramatic decline in the population was a positive asset. Instead of traffic, housing developments and endless fences we would have to contend with just the traditional obstacles of mountain and moor. Even such changes as have taken place are here of a quasinatural order; the new estates are of forestry rather than factories and the generating stations are hydro powered rather than nuclear. If one was going to restage a drove it would have to be the West Highland drove route from Skye to Crieff.

In November 1980, eighteen months after the visit to Glenelg, I sat on the portaloo on Corrour station and decided it was indeed worth a try. Corrour is not a busy station. At Euston the booking clerks either deny all knowledge of it or refuse to believe it is still operational. The nearest road is a day's walk away and the gravel track which sweeps promisingly out of the station yard forks into oblivion in less than a mile; one branch slithers into a bog and the other peters out beside a hut at the head of desolate Loch Ossian. On all sides and as far as the eye can see stretches the black and featureless moor of Rannoch.

I had walked in from Spean Bridge on a reconnaissance of the drove track round the back of Ben Nevis – fifteen miles with just one fence, two derelict bothies, many deer, some grouse and snipe, and a pair of whooper swans. It was perfect droving country. As darkness fell I had homed in on the comfortable throb of the Corrour generator as it pulsed out across the moor. *Blue Peter* was on in the empty living-room of the station master's dorran bungalow. I watched through the picture window like some furtive prowler, then felt my way up onto the platform. For some reason the generator serves only the bungalow. There should have been a candle in the waiting room but a match only lit up the startled stare of several sets of sheep's eyes. One of the ewes was actually reclining on the wooden bench.

Retreating into the night I resigned myself to a couple of hours on the portaloo. Situated at the far end of the platform, it stands well proud of the level moor, like a crow's nest. The wind now whined through the steel hawsers which guy it to its plinth and gobs of sleet began to hurtle past the open door.

The heartening thing about the day's walk had been its feasibility. From Corrour south Julia, my wife and collaborator, had already found a possible route round the Blackwater Reservoir through to Kingshouse at the head of Glen Coe; and from Kingshouse there was a choice of the old drove track or the Military road south to Bridge of Orchy and the east-west watershed into Perthshire. Assuming, therefore, reasonable weather and no more than average rainfall, anticipating too the enthusiastic co-operation of landowners – and allowing for the fact that neither of us had much idea of the pitfalls we should be looking for – I was willing to hazard that we could move cattle from Spean Bridge in the Great Glen to the Perthshire border. This was the Empty Quarter of the West Highland drove route and it looked feasible.

The timely discovery of a quarter bottle in my bag heightened the wave of euphoria. If we could manage Rannoch then surely there was nothing in civilised Perthshire that could stop us. And however precipitous the hills of Skye, Wester Ross and Inverness-shire, there were only single-day sections where, in dire need, we would not be able to find a tarmac alternative. Feasibility is important in these things. You have to believe it can be done and you have to be sure that the effort likely to be involved is commensurate with the chances of success. Sitting in the dark, glowing, I became convinced, even confident. These were two hours of sheer self-delusion but psychologically they were crucial. The obsession had become a commitment.

Next day came a letter from Gavin, a friend with agricultural expertise whose enthusiasm I had been vainly trying to arouse. He had broached the subject with a cattle farmer in Dumfries. 'At first the man laughed and laughed and laughed. "They'll just lie down and die," he kept saying. He says they'll all get lost amongst other cattle on the hill, that Glen Lyon is impossible, and that if any survive they'll be "lean as wood" and no one'll buy them.' 'I'm not trying to be gloomy,' Gavin added. 'That's what the man said.' He was not the only one.

★   ★   ★

In Fort William I waited on the landing outside a first-floor office in the High Street. Through the frosted-glass panel in the door I glimpsed a solid kilted figure segmented against a bare brown wall. He was the factor, or manager, of one of the larger estates on our proposed route and he wore hobnailed brogues. As they crunched on the lino floor they said it all. Here was a man who prided himself on the blunt approach.

In due course I shook his hand and explained my business. He knew it already; the laird had given his gracious permission and I was supposed to be just arranging the details with the factor. But he did not stop me speaking. I explained the whole project and he crunched back and forth before the forlorn office calendar. Then there was a short pause.

'Well, y'know, it won't work.' He had seen off the likes of me before. 'Ye'll never get beyond Skye, y'know that?'

'Why? What makes you say that?' I was playing the innocent but I could think of at least four excellent reasons why he was right. He had thought of them too.

'Well you just canna do it. That's all I'm saying. Cattle aren't what they used to be, y'know. These big heavy beasts today, they canna walk those distances. They've too much weight. And you'll never get them to swim. Then there's the protest. Have you thought of that now? They'll be on to you like a shot. There were no cruelty men in those days, y'know.'

I explained that the team of drovers would include a vet and that the SPCA, 'the cruelty men', would be kept fully informed. He was not interested. Indeed he was not finished. He had more 'r's to roll and more 't's to clip. There was more lino to crunch.

'The Skye crofters'll not stop you.' I gathered that he did not like the Skye crofters. 'But no one's going to let you through on the mainland. You'll maybe get permission from the like of ourselves but, y'see, it's our notion that ye'll never get this far. Lord Burton isn't going to let you wander about his ground with a herd of beasts. What about the stalking? And how are you going to hold your beasts when they make off after other cattle? I'm not stopping you. I'm just telling you. It's not on.'

He was probably right. We would proceed if only for the satisfaction of proving him wrong. There comes a point when discouragement is a positive spur.

More galling, really, were those worthies who set out to be reassuring. 'So we were going to walk the cattle. Now why should we want to do that? Aye well, if they canna go by lorry of course they'll walk. Didn't Dugal Morrison still walk his beasts over to Kyle? Aye, they'll walk all right. And swim. All cattle swim. They follow the leader, you see. And the salt

water will do them good. You'll be walking every day? Aye,
well fifteen miles a day should do it. You'll be there in a
fortnight.'

Was it really that easy? It hardly seemed worth doing. And
fifteen miles a day? I was reckoning on half that. Yet these
people were also cattlemen; they should know. In the event it
turned out that they were talking about a rather different type
of droving. But at the time so deflating were their comments
that I turned with relief to yet another school of thought on the
subject.

The mountains attract their own intelligent and partisan
incomers and although these good people may know little
about cattle they love the hills and soon acquire a fair grasp of
Highland history. Romantic notions of man and beast threading the high passes stirred them to wild and gratifying enthusiasm. Marvellous, of course it was worth doing. I mustn't
forget the Clearances, the ruined townships and abandoned
shielings, and the whole tragic tale of social oppression and
economic exploitation. And what about today's depression
and neglect? The absentee landlords, the foreign speculators,
the pockets of privilege and the discredited government agencies? Woe betide anyone who dared question our right to cross
his land. And what a perfect theme for exposing the ecological
depredations of the Forestry Commission and the Hydro-
Electric Board.

Funnily enough these ardent well-wishers had invariably
been thinking of doing exactly the same thing themselves.
Hadn't we discussed it back in '78? Or perhaps I had heard of
their plans from so-and-so? It appeared that all those who for
one reason or another did not think we were barmy were
themselves about to take to the hills with a string of beasts.
Cattle prices would rocket. By the time we got organised the
glens would be stripped of grazing and the tops would be
resounding to the bellow of marauding droves.

The world, then, was neatly divided. A third thought the
idea cruel but impracticable; another third thought it crazy but

unremarkable; and a final third thought that it was great but that it was theirs.

Who was right? I honestly did not know. We had once summered six bullocks on the field beside the house. They had trampled the rushes, eaten the grass and the butterfly orchids, tested the fences, and shown a net profit of £18.50. We had not tried it again. To all intents and purposes Julia and I knew nothing about cattle and had no idea how they might stand up to the estimated five weeks of droving. Such ignorance left scope for the imagination. Publicly I sided with those who said there was nothing to it; privately I went along with the hobnailed factor in Fort William; it wouldn't work. But even amongst those who knew about cattle – and that was just about everyone else who would be involved in the project – there was no consensus. In an unguarded moment Gavin conceded that the chances of somehow getting some of the thirty projected beasts to Crieff were reasonable, say fifty-fifty. But the chances of walking all of them all the way he put at about ten to one. And those were just the odds on the beasts. No one could vouch for the public reaction. Realistically I reckoned the chances of the thing being stopped because of unco-operative landlords or outraged animal lovers as again about evens. As the moment of reckoning approached all these odds lengthened. It might still be feasible; it was not going to be easy.

2

'Stots, stirks and stores'

THIRTY HEAD OF CATTLE

It was Dr Johnson who had put it most succinctly. 'The wealth of the mountains', he declared, 'is cattle.' In 1773 he and Mr James Boswell were making their celebrated journey to Skye; the observation came to him as they were riding down Glen Shiel. With the noble prospect of Loch Duich ahead and with the Five Sisters of Kintail rising to their right, Boswell was too excited to listen and interrupted the Doctor's chain of thought with a startling banality.

'There is a mountain like a cone,' he observed.

'No, sir,' replied the Doctor. 'It would be called so in a book; but when a man comes to look at it he sees that it is not so. It is indeed pointed at the top; but one side of it is larger than the other.'

The next peak Boswell described merely as 'immense'. But even that needed correction; it was, according to the Doctor, no more than 'a considerable protruberance'. Boswell was getting on his nerves. If only Voltaire could have come too. (He had declined, 'looking at me as if I had talked of going to the North Pole'.) The Frenchman would not have bothered him with 'considerable protruberances'; he too would have struck at the very heart of the matter, namely why it was that in the year 1773 the Highlands were still so uncivilised.

To the Doctor's way of thinking it was because the Highlands had so long been isolated from the rest of the world and the reason for this was that no one had thought the Highlands worth conquering. And what made them so undesirable?

Why, because the wealth of the mountains was cattle and cattle were movable property. Unlike crops they could always be dispersed ahead of an invader.

For the proud independence of the Highlands this is an unsatisfactory explanation but certainly the Doctor was right about the importance and the mobility of cattle. When the rest of Europe was fighting over crowns and creeds, the Highland clans were fighting over cows. In islands and glens blessed with unlimited summer grazing and very little else the rearing of cattle, and to a lesser extent sheep and goats, was an obvious means of support. Land was reckoned by the number of beasts it could feed and lairds were reckoned by the number of their retainers and the size of their herds. 'Cows' – the word was used generically to include not just breeding or dairy cows but also bulls and bullocks – were the main commodity, the main currency and the main cash crop.

They were also the main plunder. 'The stealing of cows they call *lifting*, a softening word for theft, as if it were only collecting their dues,' wrote an English officer in the 1720s. So universal was the practice that, according to another writer of the period, 'from habit it lost all appearance of criminality; they considered it as labouring in their vocation' and as 'a most wholesome exercise of youth.' The young chieftain must mark his coming of age by leading a successful cattle raid, and the dowries of his sisters were traditionally derived from the proceeds. 'To steal, to rob, to plunder with dexterity was esteemed to be the highest act of heroism' and 'a necessary public specimen of valour.'

What made the crime comparatively harmless was the very fact of its prevalence. 'The custom being reciprocally used amongst them was not reputed robbery.' Stealing sheep was a most shameful business, underhand and effeminate; but cattle were a man's sport. While the young bloods were away on a raid it was not uncommon for their own cattle to be lifted. At such times it became more a national sport than a species of warfare. There was an accepted code of practice and an accepted open season. This was late autumn when the cattle were at their strongest and still being kept on the hill grazings. The climax – the Wimbledon fortnight of the rustlers – came with the Michaelmas moon in September. 'MacFarlane's lantern' they called the moon, the MacFarlanes, like the Mac-Gregors, being mighty lifters of cattle.

Such conditions were unfavourable to legitimate trade. Before the eighteenth century evidence of the organised export of cattle from the Highlands is scant and there were restrictions on the export of Scottish beasts to England. But in the early 1700s all this changed. The 1707 Act of Union between the English and Scots parliaments removed all duties and limits on cross-border trade. In England the farmers of the home counties had just mastered the art of fattening cattle for slaughter, and abroad the troops, from Marlborough to Wellington, would show an inexhaustible appetite for salt bully beef. This demand was met from Wales, from the Scottish Lowlands and, eventually and increasingly, from the Scottish Highlands and Islands. As early as 1722 'at least thirty thousand cattle' were sold at the annual Highland tryst at Crieff, 'most of them to English buyers'. The tryst, like the lifting, took place at Michaelmas.

Not only was the demand considerable but with the defeat of the Jacobite risings of 1715 and 1745 political and economic conditions in the Highlands at last favoured the trade. After the '45 the power of the clan chiefs as represented by their rights of jurisdiction was surrendered. Compensation in hard currency created an appetite for this versatile but hitherto little-known commodity; the lairds began to charge their clansmen cash rents instead of the traditional bolls of oatmeal and pledges of unflinching loyalty. At the same time estates forfeited by the more intransigent chiefs were setting an example of agricultural improvements. Garrisons had been established at Inverness, Fort William and Fort Augustus; General Wade began construction of the first real roads in the Highlands; and cattle raiding was at last suppressed. 'Thirty years ago no herd had ever been conducted through the mountains without paying tribute in the night to one of the clans,' noted Dr Johnson, 'but cattle are now [1773] driven without danger, fear or molestation.' With the advent of banking and credit facilities the cash-based economy both favoured and necessitated the exploitation of the area's natural resources. In practice, from 1750 till 1850, these consisted almost entirely of beef cattle.

By the time Dr Johnson put his finger on the matter the annual sale of beasts had reached fifty thousand. Cattle from the west coast, the extreme north and the Hebrides could now be driven straight through the mountains, sold at the Michaelmas tryst, and driven south to England for fattening and slaughter in the following year. From Skye alone four thousand beasts were crossing by the narrows at Glenelg; in the next century this figure increased to seven thousand as the turnover at the tryst rose to an amazing hundred and fifty thousand. Falkirk, thirty miles to the south, now replaced Crieff as the main tryst, the Highland drovers thereby acknowledging their dependence on English buyers.

The economics and the geography of the drove routes were one thing. They had been exhaustively studied by Professor Haldane (in *The Drove Roads of Scotland*) and the importance of the trade could be taken as established. I was more intrigued by the practicalities and by the lore. There are still a few old-timers who have themselves done some droving and there are many with memories of ancestors who were involved in the trade. There are also a few farmers, especially on the Islands, who still move their stock short distances on foot. But talking to such people it became clear that the practicalities of long-distance cross-country droving had passed from living memory. Eighty to a hundred years have elapsed since the coming of the railways to Lairg, Kyle, Mallaig and Oban put paid to the need to walk beasts. No one could say for sure how you preserved your cattle from sinking into a peaty oblivion on the soft ground or from wearing their feet to shreds on the hard. Or how you got them to swim and to climb. Or how you kept them in peak condition when most of the feeding day was spent walking.

It was to learn these things, not to prove anything, that six would-be drovers, three dogs, three ponies and thirty head of cattle eventually assembled at the head of Loch Harport on the west coast of Skye. It was October 3rd 1981.

'Feels like the end of the world,' said Julia as we climbed out of the Land Rover into torrential rain. I thought she was talking about the weather. The gale, a nor-wester, was roaring in from the Atlantic and funnelling up the loch to stampede through Glen Drynoch and out over Loch Sligachan on the other side of the island. With the Cuillins to the south and more hills to the north the glen was in effect a wind-tunnel. We were parked, and hoping to be camped, in the field at the head of the loch and at the bottom of the glen. In other words, apart from the odd gull and perhaps a floundering fishing boat, we were the first unsecured obstructions this boisterous little hurricane had encountered. It gathered up its skirts of sea spindrift, clenched its dark clouds of heaviest rain, and came at us with devastating intent.

In fact Julia was talking not about the weather but the place. The head of Loch Harport was not the end of the road nor was it any sort of headland. But it did have that edge of the habitable world feeling; you knew there was only one way to go – back. The low ferment of cloud and the steep sides of the glen precluded any real sense of location and, encased in stiff waterproofs with cowl-like hoods, our fields of vision were narrowed to about twenty degrees. To get any impression of the place you had to swivel like a zombie and settle for disjointed slices. To the north the field was bordered by a high hedge over which were visible the bedroom windows of Glen Drynoch Lodge, the home of our hosts; above its slate roof a bracken-covered slope disappeared into the scudding cloud.

West was the loch, an aqueous grey maelstrom of sea and wind which promised the only perspective but which now repaid curiosity with instant removal of the waterproof hood. East the glen, the road and the river quickly merged into a dark blur behind the steadings and a kennel full of Gordon setters. We had come that way; for five miles there was no traffic, just a couple of houses and a lot of unkempt hillside.

The only view of any interest was to the south. Here the field sloped down to a fence with a stand of conifers in one corner. In their lee monkish figures were already beginning to grapple with a spinnaker of pristine green canvas; it was the mess tent. Between the fence and the Drynoch burn, now a wide yellow river, was another field, larger and dotted with patches of scrub and bracken. Here another monk stood, back to the wind, apparently screaming obscenities to the raging heavens. From the two black and white collies by his side I knew it was Gavin. In spite of misgivings he had agreed to come along, bringing with him the dogs plus some cattle-handling experience. For the past week he had been on Skye making last-minute arrangements and getting to know the beasts.

As I watched, his third dog broke from dead ground, disappeared into deep bracken, and then charged a thicket of brambles and willow. With a jerk a patch of dark bracken detached itself and ambled into the open. It was one of our 'boys'. From the lee of hillocks and the shelter of rush and bracken the beasts streamed into view. Twenty-nine bullocks and one cow – a small drove certainly, but a viable one, fully paid for and already much admired.

It is of course unthinkable to own a beast of the majestic Highland (or sometimes West Highland) breed without being inordinately proud of the creature. But friend and foe alike agreed that somehow we had been fortunate enough to acquire some of the best-looking bullocks in Scotland. Their horns branched impossibly wide, tapering and turning with savage beauty. When they walked their necks imperceptibly adjusted to keep the span in perfect equilibrium; it was as if they were trying to balance them. The rain was doing little for the shaggy glory of their coats but over their eyes long lank fringes hinted at shy and trusting natures. One could learn to love these beasts.

'Luckily they should be accustomed to this sort of weather,' I explained airily to Calum MacDonald, Skye's all-purpose reporter. He was vainly trying to record a piece for the radio. The tape-recorder was wrapped in a towel but the gale was snatching away our conversation long before it reached his microphone. 'They're nearly all from the west coast. Seventeen came from Barrisdale in the wilds of Knoydart. They're two-and-a-half year-olds and they're a good bit bigger than the others. Nine came from half way up Glen Coe, two from Glen Dochart and one from Loch Awe. Oh, and there's the cow. She's said to be in calf but she came from South Uist so no one is quite sure.'

I would like to have sounded like one of those dour cattlemen whose mysterious trade had lately been my obsession. But neither the jargon nor the etiquette had I mastered. Were our boys stots, stirks or stores? I shall never know. It had been hard enough deciding whether they should be bullocks or heifers. Breeders of Highland cattle do a brisk trade in purebred heifers but, for reasons that were not immediately clear, bullocks are hard to come by. Yet bullocks were certainly the ancient drovers' main fare. And they are supposedly easier to handle, heifers being somewhat wayward and flighty. Often they were beasts of three or four years old but nowadays the emphasis is on quick growth and an early visit to the abattoir. Two-year-olds were the most we could hope for.

In a frantic search I had phoned round the Highlands. Mighty lairds in Inverness, gravel-throated dealers in Stirling, dazed crofters in Wester Ross and pompous factors from Perthshire all told the same story. The bullocks were already away to the fatteners in the south; there weren't thirty in the Highlands. The Highland Cattle Society agreed, and I was about to phone round once again asking for heifers. Then, with a twist of fate for which I could claim no credit, the problem simply vanished.

The laird of Barrisdale spoke as if he had been expecting my call for weeks. His seventeen bullocks had been brought down to low ground beside the roadhead at Kinlochourn. We could see them, collect them, any time. Better still, they were as hardy, but nothing like as wild, as one would expect of Knoydart. He said they would come to his call and the rustle of a feed sack. If we couldn't drive them we could always get someone to walk in front laying a trail of cattle cobs across the hills.

He had no idea where we might find thirteen more and neither had I. But George had. George is an old and dear friend whose willingness to be involved in the drove was our one claim to the respect of the agricultural world. A stockman of wide – and long – experience, he knew more about cattle and cattlemen than the rest of us put together. But he is sparing with this fund of knowledge. I should therefore have leapt at the news that he 'knew a man in Oban'. The man's name was Hughie MacDonald. It meant nothing to me and at first I hedged at the prospect of heavy hours doing the rounds of George's Oban cronies and eventually, no doubt, being talked into the purchase of a herd of the wildest Galloways.

The first revelation was Hughie's bungalow. It was tucked away in the hills above Oban and it was as neat as a newly-wed's. The lawns were trimmed, the roses pruned and on the deep gravel stood a spotless Volvo. Hughie's initials were on the number plate. Spattered oilskins and wellington boots had surely never trespassed into this little oasis of trim suburbia. Hughie himself was equally intimidating. At the first meeting he said little. That here was the Mr Big of the west coast cattle business I no longer doubted. He seemed to have informants at every sale from Stirling to Stornoway, he had transporters, and he had grazing and feedstuffs. He, if anyone, could find the beasts, assemble them, and move them up to Skye. But would he stoop to being associated with our unlikely venture?

For an old friend – and for a generous commission – would he take on the job? His mouth opened in reply. For a long time no sound came. I had noticed this habit before; it was a good sign. Eventually, preceded and enveloped by a mighty exhalation of cigarette smoke, came the longest vowel sound ever. 'Aaaye.' It hung in the smoke-filled living room for as long as it took his wife to wheel in the tea and the cheese-spread crackers with the whisky and glasses on the lower deck. Drams were drunk, stories told, and the word went out.

Soon bullocks were being reported from all over the place. There was a herd on Jura. No one knew how many and in the event they proved too wild to be counted let alone coaxed down to the ferry. The same was true of the beasts on Rhum. They had to be tranquillised before being shipped. It was a reminder, if we needed one, of how awkward Highlanders could be. But Hughie was now firmly committed to the cause. His dour and daunting expression would dissolve into a sly and disarming smile as we talked of dealing and droving. A few years younger, or a mite less successful, and I think he would have joined us. I sensed some affinity here between the self-made dealer with his Volvo and his cattle floats and the ancient drover with his horse and his herdsmen. It was a parallel which experience of the harsher and the more romantic aspects of droving would do nothing to dispel. In trying to gain some insight into the character and calling of those who took up this noble profession Hughie would often spring to mind as the obvious modern equivalent.

In due course the seventeen Barrisdale beasts had become twenty-six, twenty-nine and thirty. We first made their acquaintance in one of Hughie's fields outside Oban. With a stick in one hand and feedsack in the other I approached with caution. Some immediately responded to a rustling of the sack. One would actually take a cob from the hand. The gentle suck of his thick pink lips bespoke profound trust and his concern not to alarm me by any sudden movement of his preposterous horns – it was as if he was rather embarrassed by them – exactly matched my own feelings about carrying a stick. Others, however, were far from tame. They simply bolted on sight. As a result, even now in the field at Glen Drynoch, there were several that I had scarcely clapped eyes on.

With the help of the dogs, and within the confines of the field, Gavin seemed able to move them all together. I watched as he took them down to the edge of the river. After inspecting the flood they shied away, scattering back into the scrub. This was worrying. The gate through which we must pass to leave the fields was on the far side of the river and there was no bridge. At a pinch drovers and dogs could be ferried across on the ponies. But cattle?

And if we got across, what then? Fields don't have fences for nothing. Beyond the gate lay open country. There was a clear run up the side of the glen and into the clouds where the maps showed the Cuillins. No fences, no dykes. A high-spirited bullock could make his bid for freedom and never be seen again. To beasts far from their native pastures, thrown together with a lot of strange companions, and menaced by humans with sticks and dogs, it must seem the obvious move. So long had we fretted over the long-term problems – of irate landowners, trigger-happy stalkers and self-righteous protesters, of beasts losing condition, tearing their feet to shreds on the hard ground or being sucked into treacherous peat on the soft – that somehow the first and most obvious danger had been overlooked. Unlike any other branch of animal husbandry, the handling of cattle rests on a gigantic confidence trick. The beasts, not their keepers, are the stronger and the faster. Even with dogs we could never hope to hold them if they had a mind to go elsewhere and never force them to tackle any obstacle against their will. It was a sobering thought. We were about to ask them for a confidence to which as yet we could stake no claim. The challenge, as I now saw it, was not whether we were going to win through to Crieff but whether we could manage the first five miles up the glen to Sligachan.

By now the mess tent was up and three bright yellow sleeping tents were being ranged alongside. The wet made them look even more garish and the wind, screaming through the conifers, swore to flatten them. At the top of the field unloading was under way. Our three Highland ponies, whose job it would be to carry loads rather than drovers, stumbled stiffly from the horsebox, sniffed the gale and then started tearing at the grass. From the Land Rover, which was mainly for carrying heavy feedstuffs, came a case of Famous Grouse Whisky. MacDonald, the reporter, accepted a dram and made for his car. He would be back on Monday for our departure. Would it still be raining then, I asked. It would. He said it, not as a tentative forecast, certainly not as a joke, but as a statement of fact.

Inside the tent hospitality was taking precedence. Although a twentieth-century cattle drove is necessarily the poorer for there being no other droves or drovers on the road, we were not destined to feel neglected. To buy a herd of cattle and to obtain the wherewithal to feed and care for them one needs capital. Capital means commercial sponsorship and to attract sponsorship one needs guaranteed publicity. Hence BBC Television's magazine programme *Nationwide* were to film our progress – if any – at various stages, and hence Matthew Gloag and Son, distillers of Famous Grouse Whisky, had accepted the brunt of the financial burden. Happily they had also undertaken to support us in kind.

The PR people and the television producer and his team were heavily committed to the success of the enterprise; they were also good friends. But they did have certain expectations and at this precise moment, wet, worried and disorganised, we were finding it difficult to sustain a pretence of unassailable confidence. When they finally departed, instead of sifting gear and sorting out the camp, the drovers laced up the tent flap and collapsed.

Chris, our vet, and JP, otherwise Jean-Pierre, the man in charge of equipment and feedstuffs, wedged hay bales round the edge of the tent by way of draughtproofing. Julia dug out a fruit cake; George opened our second bottle of the afternoon; and Gavin peeped through the flap to make sure the coast was clear. He, for some reason, had already cast the BBC as the official opposition. It was not that he resented publicity – just that he is a purist; and on such an obviously agricultural venture he was finding the company of non-countrymen unbearably intrusive. Tall and lean featured, Gavin likes to look the part. A heft hazel crook had replaced the standard issue 'cattle cane' and he was now tearing the monk-like hood off his waterproof suit. In our different ways we all subscribed to this hardy outdoor image. But only he had the confidence to sneer at an unagricultural turn of phrase or to ridicule a foam mattress. He was living the part and resented anything that did not tally with his idea of propriety.

To the drove each of us had brought his mite of experience. George was the stockman and Julia the horsewoman. Chris was a member of the Royal College of Veterinary Surgeons and JP a distinguished rock climber who knew all about camping equipment. As a lover of travel and history I was the one who had worked out the most authentic and practicable route. But Gavin's experience was altogether more glamorous. He had built roads in the Australian outback, worked cattle on the South American pampas, and sheared sheep in the Scottish borders. Now, as farmless farmer and ventureless adventurer, he was the Highland drover. He took his new role seriously; he had his reputation.

3

'Beware of Landseer'

Elsewhere in the world, cattle droving has acquired a certain romance. Texas Longhorns following the Chisholm Trail or the Overland droves in Australia have become popular legends. Highland droves evoke a different image. Here the head drover, or 'topsman', was the only one who rode; his mount was a pony rather than a horse and he never actually worked cattle from the saddle. The terrain was the decisive factor just as the weather was – and clearly intended to remain – the greatest handicap. Rain and romance don't mix. But even if Scottish droves were of humbler pretensions and of shorter duration than those in the New World they were not without excitement. Driving cattle across mountains is in fact infinitely more dangerous and demanding.

It is also more picturesque. In their attempt to romanticise the Highlands as a paradise for sport and a Valhalla for chivalry, the Victorians composed an image of the hardy Highland drover which is still current and which, like that of the cowboy, was something we had to reckon with. Sir Walter Scott and Sir Edwin Landseer were its obvious proponents. Scott's grandfather is supposed to have been a drover although he seems to have dealt in cattle rather than driven them. In the short story of *The Two Drovers* an Englishman and a Highlander fall out over a night's grazing for their respective droves. Lofty matters of principal and national pride quickly surface and the two men, notwithstanding their close friendship nor the fact that their cattle are going to suffer far more from the loss of their drovers than from the loss of a night's grass, come to blows. The Highlander stabs his rival to death and is led quietly away to the gallows.

Scott shows the simplicity of the drover's lifestyle – sleeping rough beside his beasts and sustaining himself on a few handfuls of oatmeal and a ram's horn of whisky – being more than matched by his devotion to the drove and his simple code of ethics. Highlanders were accustomed to living in the open and, combining the resourcefulness of the rustler with the exaggerated loyalty of the clansman, they supposedly valued the company of their cows more than that of strangers. In short the Highlander was a natural drover. Not surprisingly he often hired himself out to move cattle not only to Crieff or Falkirk but all the way down to England.

In *The Shepherd's Calendar* John Clare described the surprise these outlandish figures occasioned as they plodded along between neat English hedgerows.

> Scotch droves of beast a little breed
> In sweltered weary mood proceed . . .
> Followed by slowly pacing swains
> Wild to our rushy flats and plains
> At whom the shepherd's dog will rise
> And shake himself and in surprise
> Draw back and waffle in afright
> Barking the traveller out of sight
> And mowers oer their scythes will bear
> Upon their uncooth dress to stare
> And shepherds as they trample bye
> Leaves oer their hooks a wondering eye
> To witness men so oddly clad
> In petticoats of banded plad
> With blankets oer their shoulders slung
> To camp at night the fields among
> When they for rest on commons stop
> And blue cap like a stocking top
> Cockt oer their faces summer brown
> Wi scarlet tazzeles on the crown
> Rude patterns of the thistle flower
> Untrickd and open to the shower
> And honest faces fresh and free
> That breath(e) of mountain liberty

In Gaelic verse it was more often the prospect of the drover's long and painful separation from home and loved ones which offered inspiration. It also provided Landseer with a suitably sentimental theme. *The Highland Drover's Departure for the South* could, but for the abundance of background livestock, equally well have been *The Highland Soldier's Departure for the Wars*. The latter was also a favourite theme and Landseer's principal drover looks more than ready for the regiment. Kitted out in Glengarry bonnet, grey plaid, kilt, sporran, and startlingly cross-checked stockings, he dandles his bairn for the last time. A fellow drover sits on the grass whispering farewells to his lady love. The old folk grieve at the parting and a collie dog sniffs the breeze opposite some drowsy-looking rams. The morning haze lifts to reveal a deliciously blue sky.

This obviously was how it was meant to be. It was easy to sneer at Landseer but I for one would happily have swapped waterproof trousers for kilt and stockings if it meant clear skies and dry walking. As it was we had not a kilt or plaid between us. The oatmeal was reserved for the first course of breakfast and the whisky, 'an acknowledged masterpiece' according to the label, came in bottles; the bottles were in cases. But whilst envying Scott's drovers the simplicity of their lifestyle it was scarcely possible to emulate it. In those days the cattle had traditional grazing rights at every night stance – or stop-over ground – and the drovers had good friends in every glen. Moreover, they had only to satisfy their own standards of husbandry, not the more volatile expectations of the twentieth-century animal lobby. Without bales of hay and bags of cattle and pony food, without the trunks of veterinary gear and the tack and the fencing materials, a drove today would be both irresponsible and impossible.

We could, of course, have worn the kilt. The point was made by everyone from the television producer, who knew what an English audience expected of the Highlands, to Hughie the cattle dealer who wanted a good laugh. The fact of the matter was that Edward MacBean and Co. Ltd had generously provided us with the monk-like Maxproofs and no tweed manufacturer had come forward with kilts. In the spirit of drovers we took what was going. Besides I was not entirely convinced by Landseer's painting. Secretly we all hankered after his pastoral idyll and wished our 'Famous Highland Drove' (so named to give prominence to the main sponsor) was not quite so famous. But I wondered about those stockings. And about the inexhaustible bags of oatmeal.

In 1772, a year ahead of Johnson and Boswell, Thomas Pennant completed his travels in Scotland by making a tour of the Hebrides and the west coast. Pennant was a naturalist and professional traveller of high repute; he had 'a greater variety of enquiry than almost any man' according to Johnson. Like Johnson he too testified to the importance of cattle. They were 'the great support of Wester Ross', 'the only trade of the islands'. The only trade, but not the only export. For 'the proper products of this [the Isle of Skye] and all the Hebrides are cattle and *men.*' As willing emigrants and as recruits in the Highland regiments men were leaving almost as fast as cattle. It was no coincidence that Landseer's departing drover would look much like a departing soldier. Although in some areas the people were already being forcibly expelled – or 'cleared' – to make way for sheep runs, the Clearances had not yet made much impression on Skye and the Islands. There men were leaving for the same reason as their cattle – imminent starvation.

Pennant's description of the lot of the poor peasants on Skye is devastating. The short growing season, the wind, the rain, the cold and the lack of fences made arable farming nigh impossible to a southerner's eyes. For every year of bumper crops there were ten of famine. Low ground was so precious that only the rich could afford to preserve an area of pasturage to sustain their cattle through the winter. The poor tenants were 'under the necessity of keeping their cattle under the same roof as themselves' and were 'often obliged to keep them alive with the meal designed for their families'. By day the cows dragged themselves down to the shore and tore at the seaweed. There too they had to compete with their owners 'who prowl like other animals along the shores to pick up limpets and other shellfish, the repasts of hundreds during part of the year in these unhappy islands'.

> Hundreds [of people] thus annually drag through the season a wretched life; and numbers unknown in all parts of the Western Highlands (nothing local is intended) fall beneath the pressure, some of hunger, more of the putrid fever, the epidemic of the coasts, originating from unwholesome food, the dire effects of necessity. Moral and Innocent victims!

Between 1750 and 1770 the population of Skye had fallen from fifteen thousand to twelve thousand. At the same time agricultural rents had been doubled or even trebled. The lairds and clan chiefs, many of whom now lived in style in England, justified this on the grounds that cattle prices had also been rising. But they had not risen proportionately and anyway Skye was now hopelessly overstocked. In 1771 about four thousand beasts were exported to the mainland but in the following winter, a severe one, an estimated five thousand simply died of starvation.

Conditions did improve towards the end of the century. From about 1790 to 1820 Skye enjoyed a brief and golden age not of plenty but of near-sufficiency. Thanks to the Napoleonic Wars cattle prices rocketed and thanks to one of those occasional Highland bonanzas (herrings, off-shore oil or, in this case, kelp) there was ample employment. Emigration slowed and the population doubled to around twenty-three thousand by 1840. But by then the kelp industry had failed, cattle prices had fallen back and decline and destitution had again set in. Estates were changing hands at an alarming rate and both new and old proprietors looked to less labour-intensive uses of the land like sheep farming and stalking. Whole communities were being cleared and forcibly deported. By 1900 Skye's population was back at around twelve thousand.

(Today it is down to six thousand and there are less cattle on the island than were exported annually in Pennant's day.) At any given time between 1750 and 1900 conditions varied considerably throughout the Highlands. The east and north, for instance, missed out on the kelp and were 'cleared' earlier. But overall, and throughout the period, few would dispute that the general picture was one of grinding poverty, hardship and misery as a result of rack-renting and overpopulation. Most of the people most of the time went cold, hungry, dirty and destitute. Perhaps the same could be said for the inhabitants of the London slums. But the Highlands had no Dickens; instead they got Scott and Landseer. Ignoring the sordid reality these Victorians glamorised and popularised the Highlands in precisely the same way as John Ford and John Wayne have glamorised the American west. Both were frontier regions, zones of instability, anachronisms, which had not only to be settled in accordance with the norms of civilised life – the rule of law, for instance, and the laws of supply and demand – but also rendered into emotionally acceptable packages. On India's north-west frontier or in the deserts of North Africa Pathan and Bedouin posed a similar challenge. Scott's Highlander is no more faithful to reality than Flaubert's sheikh or Henty's Pathan. All are confections of an alien and blinkered society anxious to assimilate new and reluctant subjects in an acceptable manner. The real Highland drover was probably no more wholesome and noble than the real Rob Roy or the real Billy the Kid. Beware of Landseer. The drover's pristine plaid and handsome face were probably as much artistic licence as his placid tups and the cerulean sky.

All Sunday the gale blew. The tide brought monstrous waves crashing across the flats round the estuary of the Drynoch river and a hundred yards upstream its murky flood continued to explore our lower field. In the night some of the patches of scrub had become islands. Fortunately we had chosen the uppermost field for the campsite but even there the mess tent was awash. Beast as well as man evinced signs of disgust. Returning from giving the cattle their breakfast George mentioned that one of the beasts was off its food. It had a cough and seemed to move with difficulty.

'I see,' said Chris, the vet. Chris lives in Orkney but he speaks with a Lancashire accent and he always says 'I see'. If the Pentland Firth should burst into flames and Orkney be requisitioned by Beelzebub, Chris will still say 'I see'. His flat accent conveys neither indifference nor concern, just an imperturbable and universal acceptance. Trivia, miracles, brucellosis, reincarnation – Chris puts them all firmly in their place with those two dead monosyllables.

Today the syllables were flatter than ever. He, like the rest of us, was pretending not to have a hangover. What George called 'a drop of the cratur' was far and away the best attested of the drover's possessions and in this none of us was willing to question the authenticity of the popular image. Hangovers were clearly part of the acclimatisation process; they were a small price to pay for a few hours of oblivion during a damp and hostile night.

We struggled into boots and waterproofs and squelched off in search of the ailing bullock. The first heavy shower satisfactorily demolished the Sunday morning cobwebs and I noticed that what in the tent had sounded like hail was hail. On one of the Glen Drynoch Lodge chimney pots a tattered crow toyed with the gale. Every time a blast dislodged him he flapped in the slipstream of the gable wall and then beat an oblique path back to his perch. The wind was colder now. Instead of yesterday's blunt buffeting it had a touch of steel; across the glen the burns which bounded down out of the cloud were less discoloured.

There was obviously something wrong with the bullock. Even I could see that. The rest of the drove ambled over with that insatiable bovine curiosity but he just stood there looking sullen and distracted. I felt instant sympathy. Here, obviously, was a case of second sight; he had seen what lay ahead and he wanted no part of it. In the Highlands second sight is something of a commonplace. As early as 1695 Dr Martin Martin filled nearly half of his famous *Description of the Western Isles of Scotland* with instances of the phenomenon; every traveller since seems at least to have enquired into it. It is really more of a curse than a blessing in that once an event has been foreseen no human power can avert it; the die is cast. So far as I can recall, Dr Martin had taken no animal opinions on the subject. But if it is true – as we were constantly being told – that a pedigree Highland beast understands only Gaelic then surely a pedigree Highland beast may also be cursed with prevision.

I knew Chris was interested in animal psychology so I mentioned my diagnosis and awaited his opinion with interest.

'I see,' he said and asked if we could arrange a closer examination of the patient. Manhandling horned cattle in the open was something none of us relished. It was bound to come; but not yet if we could help it and certainly not when there was a perfectly good shed available in the steading of Glen Drynoch Lodge. The bullock was coaxed into it and, with much shoving and ducking from horns, George and Gavin secured a halter round its head and wedged a stob against its hind quarters.

As a precaution against various foreseeable disorders we had attempted to dose and mark the cattle in the market at Oban before they were moved up to Skye. This had involved funnelling them into a single-file 'race' for easy handling. Unfortunately the race was not designed for heads so magnificently horned. It was like trying to wheel a bicycle through an impossibly tight traffic jam. Obligingly the boys twisted their handlebars this way and that but for rather more than half it proved impossible. The present invalid was one of those who had been thus defeated; so while Chris was busy with the stethoscope I primed the guns. A thing rather like a spray for indoor plants took a viscous white liquid which spelt death to

worms and liver fluke. In cattle coming from wet west coast
pastures it was thought probable that these parasites might
already be in residence. The other gun was more like a stirrup
pump and took a 'bullet' of magnesium – actually more a shell
than a bullet, metallic and about the size of a hen's egg. Extra
magnesium is a preventative against 'staggers', an invariably
fatal condition brought on by stress and cold and said to be
prevalent at the end of the year. It sounded like a drover's
nightmare and could well explain the high rate of fatalities in
the old droves – sometimes put at one in ten. Two Rumbul
bullets per bullock meant a total outlay of about £200 but it
seemed a wise precaution.

Plugged and squirted in the mouth and with the inevitable
thermometer up its far end, the patient let out a final bellow.
Chris emerged. He made straight for the tap.

'Yes, well, it's pneumonia. That and a touch of arthritis.'
He spoke quietly as if he wanted to make sure no one over-
heard. And he was faintly grinning. I knew him well enough
to know that he was not gloating; but was he simply pleased at
having positively diagnosed the trouble? Was he savouring
some wonder-cure that he was about to perform? Or was he
just grinning the foolish grin of someone who knew that our
bluff had already been called?

To the uninitiated it sounded bad. Pneumonia *and* arthritis?
Obviously walking was out of the question; but was it already
a case for the humane killer? The idea of carrying such a thing
had struck me as negative thinking. But George and Chris had
been adamant. If a beast broke a leg miles from anywhere how
else were we both to terminate its suffering and ensure a steak
supper? There was no answer to that, although the juxtaposi-
tion of two such excellent reasons provoked a searching examination of conscience. To cherish in order to kill is the
nature of farming. Bullocks are destined for the table as surely
as ships for the sea; every step of the drove would be a step
closer to the abattoir. But I was also aware that droving – and
our little exercise in particular – might give rise to an excep-

tional man–beast relationship. If ever we got on the move it was going to be increasingly difficult to look the boys in their gentle dreamy eyes.

'I'll give him a penicillin jag and we'll keep him inside today. Check him over again in the morning. He should be all right to walk.'

I nodded knowingly. A touch of pneumonia – nothing to worry about, of course. George preferred to call it 'transit fever', a chill brought on by the long ride up to Skye. Under normal farming conditions it would probably have gone unnoticed. The patient now had his nose in a leaf of hay. One eye watched me suspiciously through his shaggy fringe. I wished I had never heard of second sight.

The rest of Sunday was devoted to domestic arrangements. On a Hebridean sabbath one keeps a low profile. We packed, unpacked, repacked, and watched the river rising.

Afternoon tea was over the hedge at Glen Drynoch Lodge. Hair brushed, waterproofs shed and the indoor world seeming strangely silent after the furore outside, we savoured already half-forgotten comforts. Stockinged feet on polished floors, Earl Grey tea in china cups, scones and blackcurrant jelly. It was exactly a month before that Gavin and I had come knocking at the front door like a couple of encyclopaedia salesmen. We had asked for a field in which to assemble the drove. We had been given two, followed by hospitality, kindness and encouragement. They said it was the most exciting thing that had happened in Glen Drynoch all year. I now looked out of the window to see their park littered with sodden tents and equipment, the ground chewed up by vehicles, and a suspicious little track leading into their cherished plantation.

Glancing up I noticed that the pall of low cloud was beginning to clot. It was almost dark and it was still raining but, like a cold that has decided to break, there was a hint of solid matter in the sky. No doubt the Gaelic has a single word that says it all. The storm had not passed, the cloud had not lifted and the weather had not broken; but there was a hint of change, a whisper of promise.

We piled into the Land Rover and headed for more creature comforts in Portree. Janet and Russell Buchanan, who had provided our ponies, were standing us a farewell dinner. So far we had had to produce only breakfast. Julia had pre-cooked enough food for a week; there was a stew in the pressure cooker and delicacies galore from girl-friends and well-wishers; and we also had a dozen little sea trout slipped shyly through the tent flap by the Glen Drynoch keeper. If this was the pattern of things to come one could see why the drovers of old carried only the wherewithal for porridge.

For dinner I had steak. It was a statement of some sort.

4

'St Bridget to keep them'

DRYNOCH TO SLIGACHAN

Although there is no manual on the dos and don'ts of cattle droving, information of a sort abounds. Every glen has its traditions: 'yon's the drovers' track, here's where they forded the burn, and in-by is the old stance, beside the public bar.' Where memory fails Gaelic tradition takes over. Fair-handed St Bridget is the patron of cattle. 'St Bridget to keep them, to watch them, and to tend, on the ben, in the glen and in the plain.'

> From the rocks, from the drifts, from the stream's rushing flow,
>   From crooked passes, from the pits where beasts die,
> From the slender ban-shee and the shafts of her bow,
>   From envy's heart and from the evil eye.

This was much nicer than the gloomy prognostications of modern cattlemen. St Bridget was on our side and I had every confidence in her dealing smartly with the slender ban-shee and the evil eye; that would leave us free to give a hand with the crooked passes and the 'pits where beasts die'. But what about those 'drifts'? Snow-drifts? Surely not in October. Yet there was another ominous reference, this time in the gathering tune of the cattle-lifting clan MacFarlane.

> We are bound to drive the bullocks
> All by hollows, hirsts and hillocks
> Through the sleet and through the rain,
> When the moon is beaming low,
> On frozen land and hills of snow,
> Boldly and heartily we go.

Now, either the MacFarlanes were going boldly and heartily about their business in the closed season or the climate was a lot different in those days. October 5th was only a week after Michaelmas and, wet and cold as it undoubtedly was in Glen Drynoch, 'frozen land and hills of snow' must surely be poetic licence.

At 6.00 a.m. the alarm bleeped. In the darkness I heard Julia wriggling out of her sleeping bag. Dressed, she backed downhill, opened the flap, and deftly slid stockinged feet into waiting boots. Then there was a pause. Her right knee pressed hard on my left temple as she wrenched at the zip of the flysheet.

'Bloody hell. It's frozen.'

Forgetting that I was pretending to be still asleep, I reached out a hand. The flysheet was crisp and responded with a creak. On closer inspection it appeared not sugared with hoar frost but caramellised with a brittle and knobbly coating of ice. Droplets of rain had simply frozen to the canvas; from outside it looked as if someone had been pelting us with frog-spawn.

Over in the mess tent George was already crouching behind a steaming kettle and a bubbling lava of porridge. He was shaming us all. Last to bed – if indeed he ever went to bed – and first to rise, he was like a ten-year-old at his first scout camp, unstoppable. From his luggage – battered brown suit-case, paint tin and ammunition box – came needles and nails, files and fencing tools, torch and teapot. For all his years he had probably spent less nights under canvas than any of us; yet he was cannily equipped. His shock of white hair, poised over the washing-up, bobbing beside a shouldered hay bale, or upside down inspecting a pony's girth, was like a beacon of excellence. We couldn't compete, only contribute.

I accepted a cup of tea and, ducking his breakfast banter, stood outside in the dawning day. A curlew cried from the lochside and a grey heron, camouflaged for the half-light, flapped lazily up the glen. Vague mists trailed through the conifer plantation and hung about the hillsides. It was still too dark to tell whether the sky was clear; but it was dry and it was still. Somewhere a dog barked and the curlew mewed again. The sounds were few and crisp, each one a revelation. The ponies snorted a morning greeting. Their fresh dung steamed with a smell as comforting as the porridge.

I hoisted a bag of cattle cobs and followed Gavin down to the beasts. By way of an experiment we had put them inside the electric fence for the night. This involved staking about half an acre with lightweight plastic poles round which were strung two strands of flimsy wire connected to a pulsing apparatus and a car battery. It seemed improbable that this arrangement would last the night. The boys liked to choose their own billet where the ground was to their liking; they had never encountered such a contemptible-looking fence and, as the wags were endlessly pointing out, hairy Highlanders were comfortably insulated whilst horned heads had to make but one flick to send the whole thing shorting into the sod. In the old days many of the traditional night stances would have been enclosed. Only on the hill would the drovers have had to set a watch through the night. We were prepared to do the same where no enclosure was available; but if the electric fence worked, so much the better.

And it had worked. Inquisitive as ever, even now a large brindled beast was gently sniffing at the wire, nuzzling it with a twitching pink nostril and turning away to inspect a pole. Whether he was impressed by the twelve volts or whether he was simply charmed by the decorative effect of the red and yellow wires was not clear. As experience would show, a paper streamer would hold them if they were in a mood to co-operate. Conversely . . .

I rolled up a section of wire as Gavin shook cobs on the ground outside. The beasts hesitated. Not till the poles themselves were removed would they gingerly saunter forth and set about breakfast. Spellbound by the morning's mystery we watched as a late-comer sniffed the linseed air and lowed. The plantation of conifers was now stilled and the whole floor of the glen seemed lulled into peaceful sleep. From the estuary came the plaintive piping of oyster-catchers. There was a harmony in the silence. The juicy crumbling of dry cattle cake, the soft suck of sodden ground and the sharp clack of horn touching horn made a pastoral symphony. Appetite is health; health too is harmony. The heron-grey light, the mist that lay low-banked up the braes, and the steamy breath that lifted lazily from sixty bovine nostrils were all one, all the same. To be so perfectly in tune with one simple moment, one barely visible spot, one prosaic event, is scarcely cause for congratulation. Ambition asks more and contentment merely teases with such fleeting joys. Yet I was happy beyond reason, savouring the seconds, denying all else, living for the music. I wanted no part in the day or the drama. Shy brown eyes were peering dreamily, questioningly at us. They were answered in kind.

Down the middle of the field the river still tugged at the long grass on the bank. It was considerably more than a burn. But it had dropped and was still dropping. I tried to wade and nearly made it, turning back where the current cut deep below the steep bank on the other side. It was a bad place to cross. Downstream the bed opened out and the current fell away sideways over a pebbly ridge. This must be the old ford. There were no steep banks and one entered the water through a thicket of rushes and scrub willow. If we could ferret the boys out of the undergrowth they would surely splash across.

Even Gavin, a man rarely given to optimistic projections, snorted approval. Jody, his star collie, would soon root the beasts out of the rushes and they would be half way to Sligachan before a camera was focused. As we walked back to the tents, concern for the crossing of the cattle gave way to personal considerations. Did one strip off to cross the river or did one resign oneself to a walk in wet attire? In Gavin's purist view of life the importance of boots looms large – not humble rubber wellingtons but traditional hill-boots of stiff leather lavished

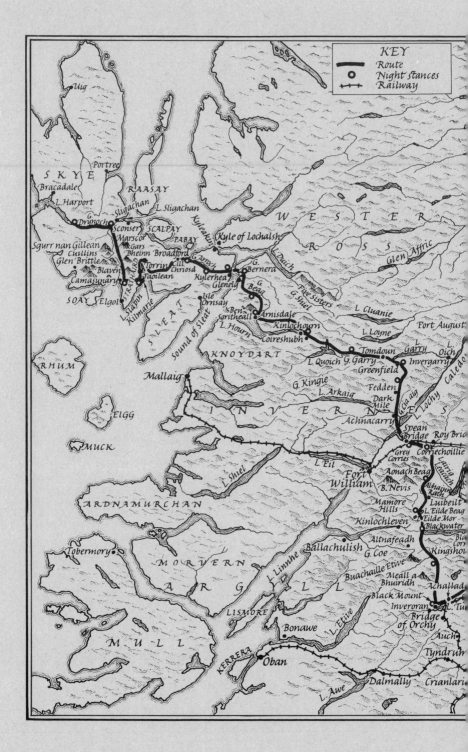

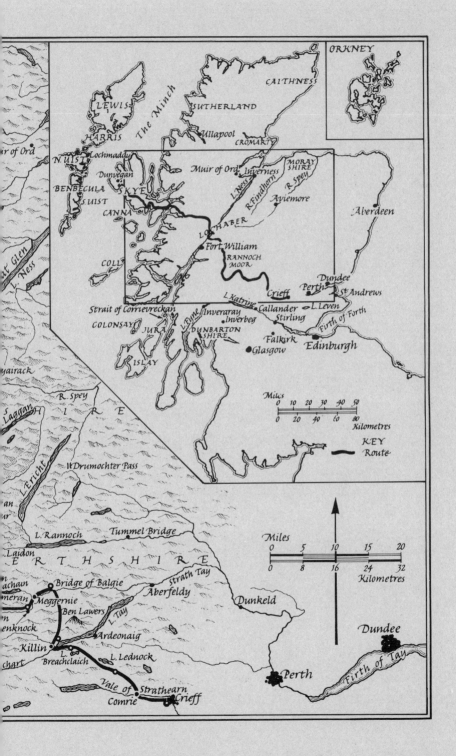

with dubbin and attention. Were these old and trusted friends to be submerged or should he carry them across? An unexpected complication was the news that his ankles had been 'replaced with meccano', the outcome of some near-fatal collision during a high-speed youth. I mentioned that, of old, the drovers' boys were described as taking off their shoes as they left home and never wearing them again until they returned. Or why not try the traditional Highland brogues, 'a kind of artless shoe' according to Dr Johnson? Like all items of Highland dress these had undergone a mysterious transformation, starting out as one-piece mocassin-like slippers and attaining a Victorian maturity as stout hand-tooled walking shoes. The only thing that you could say of both versions was that they had holes to let the water out. There must therefore be something going for perforation.

Gavin oblingingly winced at the hint of such sacrilege and, having dodged the responsibility of deciding between rotting welts and rusting joints, I grabbed a frying-pan, edged George from the cooker and set about the bacon. There was now a reassuring stir in camp. George shouldered a bale of hay for the beasts' second course, Chris was off to visit his patient, Julia was grooming the ponies and JP was clawing his way out of a nest of polythene and hay in a corner of the mess tent. It was seven a.m.; we were to leave at eight.

Three hours later the tents were down, the sun was out – *the sun was out* – and the drove was poised on the edge of the river.

'Give us the word,' yelled someone. But what was the word?

'Oh, you know, "Roll 'em out", "Perthshire here we come", "Hey up, let's move". You know.'

I did not. Anyway, the first beasts were already moving into the water and, below them, George and Julia were coaxing ponies over the pebbles. With a cheering disregard for the niceties of stage management, the drove was commencing spontaneously.

I tugged at Rona, the big grey pony, waved at Chris to ferret out any beasts still in the rushes, and stumbled into the river.

The well-wishers and the prophets of doom, the months of
doubt and the moments of panic fell away behind. With backs
to the Atlantic, the sun on our right, and the Highlands dead
ahead, all was well with the world. The sunlight danced on the
water and the pebbles shifted beneath our feet. Behind us was
a sodden and trampled field; ahead lay two hundred miles of
pastures new. It was a good feeling. For a moment I indulged
in a glimpse of the future. The challenge was still just to get to
Sligachan, five miles up the glen. But the reward was weeks of
challenge-free roaming round quiet fjord-like lochs, of breasting eerie passes with stags clattering on the rock, and of treading the open moor as the sun dipped behind a heathery horizon.
And all this – but not only this – got nearer with each stride.

In front a red phalanx of bullocks was now surging out of
the river and across the lush Drynoch turf. Gavin was upfront
calling his cohorts, the gate was wide, and beyond beckoned
the freedom of the glen, the open island and the fenceless
Highlands. Suddenly space held no threat. There was a dogged discipline about the beasts which suggested they knew
precisely what was expected of them. The collies flew along
the flanks in a frenzy of excitement and the ponies valiantly
adjusted to laden pack-saddles and bulging panniers. So much
determination would not easily be denied. There was an inevi-
tability about it all, a 'rightness', an overwhelming sense of
having precedent and propriety firmly on one's side. It
dwarfed all else and, as I searched the hill for a reason, I saw,
at last, the Cuillins.

'One always hears of Highland scenery at its best; one usually
sees it at its worst.' This was not Dr Johnson but an American
lady, Elisabeth Pennell. An inveterate traveller, she toured the
Hebrides on behalf of *Harper's Magazine* in 1888. Neither she
nor Joe, her husband, enjoyed the experience. 'We have no
hesitation', she wrote, 'in saying our trip to Scotland was the
most miserable we ever made.' The climate was appalling, the

travelling abominable, the people 'the most downtrodden on God's earth', and the scenery invisible. It goes without saying that they coincided with a period of acute social distress and with a summer of excessive rainfall. Neither is exactly exceptional and amidst the romantic outpourings of other nineteenth-century travellers Mrs Pennell deserves to be applauded for her brutal frankness. A glimpse of the Cuillins is not vouchsafed to every visitor; it can even take Sghianachs by surprise.

For the record, Dr Johnson in an otherwise classic account of Skye fails to mention any 'considerable protruberances' at all, whilst James Boswell's brief note – 'a prodigious range of mountains capped with rocky pinnacles in a strange variety of shapes' – sounds more like hearsay than personal observation. The two travellers passed right round the Cuillins but, once again, the weather was against them.

They were also innocents in the matter; they were sampling nature with untutored palates. One easily forgets that before the Lake Poets discovered virtue and beauty in uneven ground there was no obligation to burst into hyperbole over a wilderness. Writing in the 1720s Edmund Burt, an English officer stationed at Inverness, actually preferred his mountains decently shrouded in cloud. For their true outlines were 'extremely harsh to the eye . . . and the clearer the day, the more rude and offensive they are'. Nor did he appreciate their colouring – 'of a dismal gloomy brown drawing upon a dirty purple; most of all disagreeable when the heath[er] is in bloom'. 'Their stupendous bulk, frightful irregularity and horrid gloom' were alike repulsive, a blemish on the face of the earth and a challenge to the very notion of civilisation. It was not till 1803 when William and Dorothy Wordsworth toured the Highlands with a reluctant Samuel Taylor Coleridge that this attitude was questioned; it was finally routed by Sir Walter Scott, a century after Burt and a half century after Johnson and Boswell.

By contrast, our modern palates are distinctly jaded; we are

suffering from a surfeit of mountains. Burt had thought it the
height of absurdity when some of his fellow officers 'took it in
their fancy' to try and scale Ben Nevis; and the Wordsworths
would surely have frowned on anyone aspiring to a perspective
which dwarfed the contours of their inspiration. But by the
1870s things were changing. 'Cragsmen' and 'Alpinists' had
established a rationale of their own and it was in fact the
Alpine Club's discovery of the Skye Cuillins which first lent
respectability to Scottish mountaineering. Now, after a century of belays and bivouacs and after an avalanche of climbing
books, the mountains hold few surprises. To readers steeped
in epics of Himalayan endeavour, to ears accustomed to the
new vocabulary of aiguilles and arrêtes, bergschrunds and
verglas, and to eyes seared by ever more dazzling colour prints
on ever more glossy art paper, a few much-hiked pocket peaks
on a Hebridean island should prompt no great stirring of the
spirit.

Yet the Cuillins still work their magic – still retain the
capacity to take one by surprise. Seen on that bright October
morning poking above the gilt and grassy slopes of Glen
Drynoch, their ferocity was shocking. New snow veined the
highest slopes and zig-zagged across the cleft faces. It gave a
keen edge to the saw-tooth ridges and flew in spindrift from
the jagged pinnacles. Fleecy clouds sailing in on the breeze
were being ripped and sundered, while unexplained mists
foamed and billowed below them. The elemental violence of it
all was emphasised by the pastoral calm of the glen. It was
their sheer improbability that impressed. I have been lucky
with mountains – a distant glimpse of Nanga Parbat's bulk, a
close-up of Rakaposhi's symmetry and a vision of ethereal
Kanchenjunga. Today I was taken unawares by a cameo of the
Cuillins.

'Skye's major asset. They call them the only real mountains
in the British Isles.' Calum MacDonald, Skye's mediaman,
had popped out of the bracken and greeted me like an old
friend. Today, instead of the tape-recorder, he brandished an

enormous antique press camera with one of those exploding head-lamps for a flash. He was now, he explained, covering the story for one of the Scottish dailies. But his radio conscience evidently pricked; at Kylerhea, where we planned to cross to the mainland, he would be back with the microphone – 'to cover the woman's angle with Julia'.

'You were wrong about the rain then,' I said. He looked blank and I reminded him of his forecast. But of course he remembered; it was just that he had not registered that the rain had stopped. For this revelation he was genuinely grateful; he unzipped his anorak and sped off down the glen, suddenly reminded of a host of dry-day commitments.

The sun had also brought out the sight-seers. Cars were lazily leap-frogging along the main Dunvegan road on the other side of the glen; there was a bus bristling with telephoto lenses. Some were tourists, others had come to appraise the beasts, Highland cattle being now practically unknown on Skye. And there were also those who came to see how we were making out. All the world loves a loser and they had the possibility of six in one frame. We could lay no claim to the sympathy and prayers that would have been bestowed on the departing drovers of old. Tearful farewells and heavy hearts were out of the question. We were doing it all backwards, fleeing from a sodden field instead of a warm hearth and heading homewards instead of away. Under any other circumstances the incredulous crofters could reasonably have called us cowboys. Where was the pathos of that Landseer parting? The occasion was the poorer for its absence and though the drove felt right enough an awful lot was demonstrably wrong. Only the massive uncertainties ahead lent plausibility. I bore no grudge against the pessimists because without them the nagging sense of futility would have got out of hand.

Three miles up the glen the invisible track, which I had confidently claimed as a drove road, recrossed the Drynoch burn, merged with the tarmac of the A863 and a mile later took off left over a peaty shoulder. The burn was no problem.

Drovers cursed, ponies floundered and dogs splashed but the beasts waded confidently across. We paused on the other side. Julia produced toffees, Gavin a thermos. George was muttering something about the dogs running the beasts off their feet and both he and Chris were concerned for yesterday's patient.

'It's not right, that beast, Chris. See the leg there. Aye and there's the cough.'

'I see,' said Chris. I, on the other hand, did not see. I was not even sure which beast they were talking about. As yet they all looked identical and if the odd cough meant pneumonia then we had at least a dozen cases.

We hit the road in style. JP was waiting in the Land Rover and took the lead with warning lights flashing. Gavin, knee-deep in collies, kept just ahead of the cattle who, with the occasional reminder from Chris and me, bunched obediently to the left of the white line. George and Julia took up the rear, each leading a pony along the grass verge. All in all it was a respectable display – a 'cattlecade' as the papers would have it.

Curiously highways, excluding motorways, are the one place where cattle have as much right as people. There is, I am told, no law of trespass in Scotland. Moreover, according to the Department of Agriculture, there is no restriction on the movement of cattle; the Highlands are brucellosis free. But this does not mean you can take your cow wherever you want. Far from it. Mountains, moors, forests and foreshore – not to mention fields and grazings – are all owned by someone and though deer, hikers and outward-bounders may roam at will, cattle and ponies may not. The same goes for footpaths, tow paths, bridle paths and even, if I understood the solicitors right, drove roads. Reference to Lord Deas's judgement in Jenkins v. Murray ('vide pages 336–7 in Rankine on Land Ownership') might, they suggested, clarify the situation but basically recent precedent counted for everything. Unless a drove road had been used for droving at least once in the last twenty years, we – or rather the beasts – had not a leg to stand on. 'It is essential', the solicitor's letter had concluded, 'that you obtain the formal consent of all the owners of land over which you propose to drive the cattle and also obtain insurance cover in respect of any damage caused during the cattle drove.'

The letter made no mention of public roads but its tone was enough to discourage further legal research. Instead I phoned the local police station. The desk officer was a fund of information. The cattle must not completely block the traffic; there must be a man in front and another behind; and there must be no droving after dark. Gates to adjoining properties should be closed and he earnestly recommended giving a wide berth to vegetable gardens, rockeries and herbaceous borders. Did that mean it was all right to use the main road? Indeed it did, it was a public road wasn't it? It would be polite to contact the Chief Constable in each region and this I did. One promised to alert his local officers and another said an escort car would be waiting. Had tarmac not been so hard on cloven feet and had we not been committed to retracing the traditional drove routes I would have been tempted to take the main road all the way to Crieff.

Without as yet glimpsing a policeman we swung smartly left onto the moor. The traffic accelerated away leaving the wet tarmac glistening like a strip of patent leather. Only a spattering of dung attested our passing. When I looked back at it, Glen Drynoch revealed the regularity of form which is its chief characteristic and which for the past two days it had so successfully kept hidden. Between straight parallel walls its floor sloped evenly and gently down to the Atlantic waters of Loch Harport, a giant's slipway with the river a slack hawser lashed to the capstan of the Cuillins and awaiting some gargantuan barque. Not the most picturesque of glens perhaps but 'interesting and comparatively fertile' according to Joseph Mitchell, the man who built the first road down it. It was 'interesting' because in 1823, two years before his visit, it had been 'cleared of tenantry to the number of 1500'.

The ruined cottages and green spots of the once cultivated crofts were to be seen scattered on the hillsides, indicating the sites of the abodes of the expatriated families; but all then was solitude and nothing was heard by the traveller but the bleating of sheep. The laird in this case, instead of living amongst his people, resided in a distant part of the country and spent large sums in futile parliamentary contests . . .

Today the population must be less than a dozen. Hens once cackled here, cows browsed on the hillside, children played by the burn. But look again and the imagination falters. To animate such tranquil desolation is impossible. It was not a lambish bleat but the baa of an old ewe, sharp, bronchial and melancholic, which now protested our presence from the encroaching bracken. The place was hers, didn't we know? Cattle? Men? All trespassers.

Ahead two brimming ruts threaded a maze of peaty puddles and disappeared over the horizon like railway tracks. I imagined the map of Ontario with the Canadian Pacific Railroad weaving through the lakes. But here the week-end downpour had just added a few critical inches to the water table. We rounded a knoll that was now an island and saw the ruts plunge into an ominous oblivion of bog cotton and green slime.

Only Gavin had walked this section of the route. He was now out in front, his face unavailable for inspection. His stride, though, grew more purposeful, even self-conscious, as he forged manfully ahead. The bog cotton bobbed, the collie in front started to paddle, and the matted vegetation shuddered; then it bowed as the green slime closed over his precious boots. No one laughed. He waded on, struck firm ground, and slowly rose from the deep, slurping forward a further fifty yards for good measure. Then the casual glance behind, the look of pained amazement at our hesitation and, hands on hips, the weary 'oh do come on'; it was brilliantly done.

The beasts, unconvinced, had halted. Drovers scoured left and right for a more promising ford and others rummaged through the pony panniers. We had invested in a hundred yards of stout rope and some long stobs (fence posts) specifically for extricating beasts stuck in bogs. They were in the

1 The Drovers:
John and Julia Keay,
George Knight,
Russell Buchanan,
Gavin Douglas and
Jean-Pierre de Rohan.
Missing:
Chris Wiper, vet

2 'The Highland Drover's Departure for the South' by Sir Edwin Landseer

trailer; the trailer was attached to the Land Rover; and the Land Rover was by now at Sligachan. We had not so much as a dog lead.

My diary – it hardly qualifies as a log – scribbled in the heat of the moment, records intense concern. The Jeremiahs had conditioned us to expect disasters and our own ignorance preyed on this fear. Compared to what lay ahead such an obvious and innocent little obstacle scarcely rated. Yet I suspect that we were nearer to real danger even than we thought. For, apart from George, none of us had yet learnt what might be identified as the first principle of droving – namely that the cattle are cannier than the drovers.

On Himalayan glaciers they send the yaks on ahead. I had read it in a book. Yaks beat a good path through soft snow and, more to the point, they have an instinctive faculty for detecting hidden crevasses. On the same principle Highland cattle know a thing or two about bogs. Much anxiety might have been avoided had we appreciated this; but it was not until we got among the black and treacherous peat hags of Rannoch Moor that the lesson would be learnt. With respect to the Jeremiahs, I now find it hard to believe that a Highland cow ever stumbled into a bog unless its natural caution had somehow been numbed by fright.

Alas, when beasts know their drovers no better than the drovers know their beasts, fright is easily induced. Hounded by wild shouts and waving sticks, a blond and bony bullock – not one of our prize specimens – bounded into the mire and, instead of crossing it, proceeded to explore it. Sinking even deeper and kicking like a rodeo steer, it plunged to its belly, then miraculously reared onto a wobbly tussock, plunged in again, apparently stuck fast, and then laboriously repeated the whole performance before rejoining its brethren. I doubt whether we could have lost it; it was not a heavy beast and there were plenty of willing hands present. But the scare was real. Obviously this was one of those 'pits where beasts die'; and obviously St Bridget was on our side.

5

'Wild and desolate beyond conception'

SLIGACHAN THROUGH THE CUILLINS TO CAMUSUNARY

'The beasts is doing fine, John, just fine. Let them take their time. No good pushing. Just leave them be. They're doing great. Och yes. Just great. Now, what do you call this place?'

'Sligachan, George, Glen Sligachan.'

'Och well, that's fine. Aye, fine.' Pause. 'And how's your bottle?'

'Haven't touched it.'

'Well then, will we take a dram? Drop of the cratur, eh? Beasts is needing a rest.'

It was eleven a.m.; the rain looked like settling in. With touching concern our sponsors had responded to the danger of drovers being unavoidably distanced from the communal supply by coming up with individual rations – a daily distribution of quarter bottles. Vowing ever to honour the name of Matthew Gloag we unscrewed and drank in unison.

'See that, John. Yon beast with the head. Ah now, see that. What do you think then? Cuddin', eh? Aye cuddin'. That's a thing now. Beasts is doing great.'

We lolled on the heather and peered through the dense drapes of rain. The grey rock that swirled towards the invisible summit of Sgur nan Gillean was already streaming. The burns were rising, the waterfalls roaring. Yet the boys did indeed look content. For three hours they had virtually grazed their way forward, fanning out in a wide arc to wade through the heather and browse on its tender shoots. Across the little hollows of sheep-cropped grass they strolled with a purpose, pausing only to tug at a straggly bog myrtle. Then back into the jungle of heather, tails swishing, noses deep in the shrubbery, twisting and munching in an ecstasy of indulgence.

'Where are those film boys now, eh? The beasts is cuddin'. I'd like the people to see that. Those cruelty men and the like. You'll no see cattle more contented than that.'

He rubbed a stubbly chin, pushed back his flat cap and launched into a long reminiscence about his days as head stockman at the Oban mart. In an expansive mood, with his feet in dry socks, and the horizon empty of all possible detractors, George is the best companion in the world.

For all concerned the day had begun well. We had camped at a junction of the glens at the head of Loch Sligachan where, in the old days, the droves from the Outer Hebrides which had landed at Dunvegan, Bracadale and Drynoch would have been joined by those coming from Portree and the north of Skye. To the east, hills fell steeply into the loch with the road to Broadford ringing the base of the cone-like Glamaig. South our track to Sligachan struck off through the heart of the Cuillins while west lay a path over to Glen Brittle plus yesterday's road from Loch Harport. Camp was beneath the road north to Portree and beside the boisterous waters of the loch. The sun had risen on a neat little stance with tents trimly dressed on the level turf. The camp-fire still smouldered and puppy waves lapped playfully on the shore of Loch Sligachan. Better still, the electric fence was intact, the beasts were ready for breakfast and the drovers ready to move. By eight o'clock the cattle had crossed the bridge at the head of the loch and turned into Glen Sligachan to cut through the Cuillins.

Admittedly there were no longer thirty beasts. For our own peace of mind as much as anything, Chris had prescribed a short convalescence for the pneumonia patient. He was to be taken by trailer to a cosy field in Broadford, there to await our arrival, by a circuitous route, in five days' time. Predictably it was JP, our unofficial conscience, who announced that at a drop-out a day we would be herding phantoms by the time we

reached Rannoch. But this early reverse was tempered by a
pleasant surprise over the ease with which the invalid – and,
for company, a friend – were detached from the rest of the
drove and then without the benefit of handling pens safely
coaxed into the trailer. Each day Chris would now have to find
time for a dash into Broadford to administer the daily injection
– another handling problem. But in retrospect his decision
proved a wise one. Given a say in the matter it seems probable
that not a beast in the drove would have resented a daily jag to
be excused the confusion that lay ahead.

'Ho-ho-ho-ho-ho.'

'Caaaaalm on, caaaaaalm on.'

We were off again, me charging through the heather from
beast to beast like Wee Willie Winkie – I thought it showed we
meant business – while George ambled towards a selected
coterie of cud-chewers clicking his tongue. Already, though
not without hours of patient observation, he had divined the
decision-makers. The beast that fed first, that stayed in the
lead the longest, that cherished its body space the most, was
the one to watch for. When several struck out on their own,
which would the majority follow? It was thought crucial for
the success of the drove to identify a leader and, having done
so, to uphold his – or her – authority. I only hoped that no
one was making a similar appraisal of the drovers.

At this point there were four contenders for bovine sup-
remacy. George, perhaps allowing gallantry to overrule his
better judgement, favoured the solitary cow, Matilda. It was
he who had so named her and in deference to his improbable
devotion the name stuck. But Matilda did not reciprocate.
During a long and chequered relationship she showed her
champion no favours. Nor did her personal charms in any way
excuse this ungrateful conduct. With horns that splayed like
Easyrider's handlebars, eyes that glared fiendishly, a coat that
was a disgrace to her breed, and a gait worthy of a camel,
Matilda was the one beast that even I could identify. To
everyone's embarrassment she was unmistakable and, as befit-

ted one so ill-conceived and underrated, she duly became our mascot. But she was also a maverick, wilful, cussed and incorrigible. Her age was uncertain, her pregnancy uncertified and her pedigree doubtful – facts of which we would have frequent cause to remind her. The kindest thing that could be said of her was that she came from South Uist. In those wild and wayward eyes lurking behind a lank, seaweed fringe lay a hint of the further Hebrides. She belonged to a ten-acre croft with a foreshore to roam on and a gale for company. She didn't go for society; it was not her fault.

The idea of having a cow was that an older more experienced beast would naturally assume the leadership. The idea was good and in so far as Matilda would clearly never be content to follow she appeared a born leader. But unfortunately she rarely took any beasts with her – I suspect that she in fact forbade them to come – and anyway never led in the right direction. Even now, as we plodded ever deeper into the gloom of Glen Sligachan, we were covering more ground in pursuit of the old lady than of all the other beasts put together. Today she seemed to have a heavy list to the right, the west. Was she hankering after home? Drawn to the burn for a drink? Or after making an attempt on the Cuillin ridge? Nothing so foolish. As we forged on, it became clear that her sudden sideways excursions were prompted by a canny reading of the terrain. From the steep flanks of Marsco moraines spilled onto the floor of the glen intersecting the path. Little rivulets of loose stones, they were not to Matilda's liking; hence the determined attempts to outflank them. Her distaste for a loose footing was obvious at every minor burn. The water was now rising fast and all would soon be impassable; but Matilda was not to be hurried. She chose her own ford and with each leg in turn gingerly probed the stony bed before transferring any weight. George was filled with admiration; I looked at my watch.

We had five hours till dusk but, having managed to forget the map, I had no idea how much ground remained to be covered. Sundry well-wishers, including a persistent photographer, had long since turned back and would by now be drying off in the bar of the Sligachan Hotel. Julia and the ponies had disappeared into the murk ahead; and although Gavin was supposedly still up there somewhere it was a while since our last sighting. Meantime the rain was coming on in earnest, the glen growing tighter and darker. The quarter bottles were empty.

Glen Sligachan has a reputation for crushing the spirit. 'Wild and desolate beyond conception,' thought Alexander Smith, 'compared to which Glen Coe is Arcady.'

> The scenery repels you and drives you in on yourself. You have a quickened sense of your own individuality. You hardly dare speak lest you be overheard. You can't laugh. You wouldn't crack a joke for the world . . . Glen Sligachan would be the place to do a little bit of self-examination in.

Poor Smith had little time for self-examination. A lace pattern designer from Kilmarnock, he had been precipitated to celebrity on the strength of his verses some of which were much admired by Edinburgh's literary lights in the 1850s. Not all though. Smith was accused of plagiarism and lampooned as one of the 'Spasmodic poets'. Today it is his prose which is more congenial, especially his account of a holiday in Skye, the birthplace of his wife. It was published in 1866. The following year, aged thirty-seven, he died 'of overwork and trying to support a family on a writer's income'. There was a lesson there.

According to Smith the lochan just over the watershed at the head of Glen Sligachan would come as a relief to the eye. I begged to differ as, with just three hours till dusk, we transferred from the slopes of Marsco to the still steeper sides of Bla Bheinn (Blaven). The glen had become a tight corridor of rock between whose walls the cloud clamped ever lower. Unseen, the scenery could yet be heard and felt as waterfalls clattered among the rocks above and a sudden blast of wind and rain told of some desolate side corrie. The sense of oppression was everywhere heavy with menace. Those black waters of the lochan were surely meant for drowning maidens in. Chattering Gothic monsters should line the ledges beyond and the laughter of a robber chief echo down the galleries on high. It was no place for placid cattle and they tossed their heads and twitched their tails in disapproval.

Although Matilda's attempts to outflank the moraines were now frustrated by their falling straight into the lochan, our forward progress had become pitiful. Scrambling up and down the mountainside in search of a crossing of the endless burns, we were making more ground laterally and vertically. George no longer cooed over the cattle nor begged a rest for them every half mile. With tongue and stick he was revealing a whole new persona as, exhausted, man and beast neared tether's end.

At one point the path – I had stopped kidding myself it was an old drove route – wriggled up a cliff by way of rocky outcrops and runnels of scree. The rock was bare, the scree loose and the cliff fell into the loch. Without quite realising the danger we worked the beasts towards it in single file. Then George kept them coming while I perched just below the worst stretch, ostensibly to prevent them bunching but actually just mesmerised by the horror of it. At eye level I watched 112 cloven feet scrabble on the scree and then clatter on the rock. Each slip jarred the nervous system like a stylus skidding on a record. It seemed – it probably was – suicidal.

Cursing the fact that, with six drovers, only two of them were around when they were needed, I bellowed for Gavin; no answer. Two figures were just visible on the skyline but on closer acquaintance they turned out to be strangers. Not even George could muster a quip. We pounded past, too wet and too furious even to rejoice at the easier going. Through the mist the Land Rover at last materialised beside, and dwarfing, a bothy on the shore of Camusunary Bay. Though small and forlorn the bothy had a roof and windows. Gavin had painted a glowing picture of its comforts and I did not doubt he and the rest were already savouring them.

In the fading light, another unknown figure barred our path. We were now a mere stone's throw from the bothy door and its promise of hot soup and a release of righteous remonstration.

'What's this then? Maxproofs? Wellie boots? That's not what they wore y'know.'

It was a man's voice with a North of England accent.

'And yer cattle aren't right neither. Should be black y'know. Black cattle, that's what they had in the old days.'

It was just a bit of friendly ribbing; he was probably envious of us. He had at least taken the trouble to come out and see us in. But at the time I could not see it that way. I made my feelings clear. The unknown figure retreated into the gloom.

He may, it appears, have been a member of the Newcastle constabulary. If we had high hopes of the bothy, so too, I was quickly informed, had a young German couple, thirteen Geordie policemen, and a sad-looking girl. After delicate negotiations the policemen had been prevailed upon to make way for the drovers. They knew of a cave and would sleep there. I decided to keep quiet about my rencontre outside. The Germans, however, stood their ground; the firewood was theirs and hence also the fire which roared invitingly but out of reach. As for the girl, she was evidently a permanent resident. Her brown rice and lentils were steaming by the fire and a shawl and beads hung from the blackened beams. Having cadged a cigarette she deftly extracted the tobacco, put most of it in an envelope and rolled the remainder in her own papers.

By now I was spluttering with rage. Why hadn't someone come out to help us? Why hadn't they at least got the fence up for the beasts? And where indeed was the soup? JP tried to change the subject. He had managed to drive over the ridge from Kilmarie which, I was to understand, was no small achievement; as a result we did at least have the tents. I noticed only that in the process he had bent the fender of our brand-new but borrowed Land Rover. Unhappily Gavin, who had made all the ground arrangements on Skye, chose this moment to complain that we were taking people for granted.

The cattle were in the wrong place, the Land Rover had chewed up the grass, and tomorrow we could not even cross the ridge without first going to see the factor of the estate.

'Frankly, John, we can't go on like this.' Like what? He seemed to have assumed the role of conservation officer for the shy and uncorrupted natives of Skye; we were just a load of cowboys stampeding across their gentle Gaelic sensibilities with ne'er a backward glance for the consequences. It was nonsense and I told him so.

On reflection the final straw was that jibe about the cattle not being black – a small point, admittedly, but a sore one and one about which we held strong views. 'The black cattle of Argyll', 'the black cattle of Skye', 'the trade in black cattle from the Scottish Highlands' – almost invariably the Highland drovers of the eighteenth and nineteenth centuries were described as dealing in cattle of just the one colour. And from the descriptions, these black cattle were clearly not sleek Aberdeen Angus or frisky Galloways but genuine Highlanders, short of leg and long of horn and hair. They were sometimes called 'kyloes', possibly to differentiate those that came from the islands by way of the kyles, or straits, and they were certainly smaller, lighter beasts than the modern Highlander. Such considerations lay behind the sceptic's insistence that today's heavy red Highlander could never approach the feats of locomotion performed by its nimble black forebears.

There are today still black Highlanders. They are not noticeably smaller than their red cousins and they are extremely rare and hard to come by. Knowing this much – and anticipating the jibes – I am ashamed to admit that we had briefly toyed with the idea of Galloways. Eventually it was Dr Johnson who resolved the problem. 'He that travels in the Highlands may easily saturate his soul with intelligence, if he will acquiesce in the first account.' The second would, however, inevitably contradict it. Thus on Skye a 'deer forest' would turn out to have neither deer nor trees, a crofter's township would have no streets, and his 'black house' might turn out to be green. By the same token might not his cattle turn out to be something other than black? All one had to do was prove it.

Fortunately evidence – and in a matter so sensitive who could forbear to parade it? – turned out to be plentiful. 'The true West Highland breed are of various colours, black, dun, brindled and brown; but the black is the most common . . .' writes the author of a compilation on the agriculture of Argyll in 1798. Ten years later the author of a similar work on the Hebrides takes the same line: 'a bull of the kyloe breed . . . should be black (that being reckoned the hardiest and most durable species) or dark brown, or reddish brown without any white or yellow spots.' Note here that black is the ideal but, by implication, not necessarily the most common. The author of the comparable report for Inverness (which then, as now, included Skye) having declared the Skye cattle 'superior to anything of the kind known in Britain, perhaps in the world', chose not to pen his own description of them but to quote from the poet Alexander Campbell.

Kintail's famed breed, or that of Skye's green isle
Are deemed the best – low stature, thick curled pile;
Spine long and straight, ribs deep, high crested, strong;
Let those true forms be found your herd among;
So will they thrive when led to southern keep,
And prove more gainful far than *alien* sheep.
From *The Grampians Desolate*, 1804

Campbell was speaking out on behalf of cattle and against the new craze for sheep. His partiality was not for a particular colour or conformation but for Highland cattle as a whole. In the notes to his poem he achieves the most vivid and relevant description of the 'famed breed' to be found anywhere.

A cow of the Skye or Kintail breed is a remarkably handsome animal; it carries its head erect, which gives it a deer-like air peculiar to the cattle of those districts. Besides, a straight, thick back, deep in the rib, elevated head and neck; blue or clear yellow horns tipt with black and sharp pointed, the hide of a *dark brown colour* [my italics], short legs and large bushy tail – are marks truly characteristic of a cow, ox or bull of the real Highland breed of black cattle.

Dr Robertson, author of the Inverness report, adds an even more relevant observation to the effect that although the richer lairds took pride in their herds the poorer tenants scarcely bothered about such niceties of breeding and there were therefore many exceptions – exceptions, that is, not to the cattle being black, but of a 'dark brown hide'.

Throughout the nineteenth century 'black cattle' continued to be of many colours and if anything grew less black. H. H. Dixon, author of *Field and Fern or Scottish Flocks and Herds*, toured the Highlands in the 1860s and visited most of the best Highland herds. Lord Dunrobin's were 'dun and brindled', the Duke of Atholl's included yellows, duns, reds and dark reds (but no mention of blacks) and the leading breed of 'Argyllshire Blacks' at Poltalloch were mostly dun or brindled. True, Youatt's standard work on cattle breeds insisted that the proper colour of the 'West Highland' was black, but in *Cattle Breeds and Management* (1897) William Housman pounced on this, noting that the contributor was an Islay breeder and inferring that like all breeders he favoured the colour of his own herd to the exclusion of others. 'Red, yellow-red, yellow, dun, brindled, silver dun and a silvery sort of white are all proper colours of the true breed' and although in some places black was preferred, in others red etc. held the field. In Sassenach eyes these other colours were seen as definitely 'more suited to the English park landscape'. Of eighteen entries in the Jubilee Show of the Royal Agricultural Society in 1889, nine were red, five yellow, one dun and three black.

By this time the reputation of the breed was suffering. Dairy cattle were gaining in popularity in Islay and Kintyre while other breeds (Shorthorns, Galloways, Ayrshires and Herefords), under the auspices of their breed societies, were being dramatically improved and winning respectability and publicity. The poor Highlander was in danger of being relegated to the status of a crofter's mongrel. In defence of 'the famed breed' Island farmers, Highland lairds and Perthshire noblemen closed ranks and at last agreed on joint action. In 1884 the Highland Cattle Society was formed and in the following year produced its first herd book which listed all bulls then known to exist. These listings confirm the impression already gained; less than half the bulls were black. In a carefully phrased preface the editing committee conceded that 'the usual colours are black, brindled, red, yellow and dun' but added that 'there is considerable difference of opinion among breeders as to which is preferable'.

Whether the breed was native to the Highlands (i.e. descended from indigenous wild cattle) the committee could not decide. But if this proved to be the case they believed that it would be found that there were originally two true strains. One, the kyloe or West Highlander of the coast and Islands, was probably predominantly black; the other, the Mainland Highlander, was probably not.

Given that in the last hundred years the black colour has been practically bred out of existence while average weights have increased by some thirty per cent, it is obvious that selective breeding can have dramatic results. But so, equally, can that neglect of the niceties of breeding which necessity often imposed. Only a small percentage of the drover's beasts would have come from large well-managed herds and thus whatever fashion or fancy may have decreed as the desirable colour at any given time or place is not conclusive. In short, 'black cattle' was a generic term and a term of convenience, not a description. In the eighteenth century and especially in Argyll and the Islands black beasts may have outnumbered the rest; but not in the nineteenth and not in the rest of the Highlands. As with Highland tartans and clans and as with Highland reels and gatherings, I suspect that the regulation of Highland cattle had a lot to do with the Victorians' passion for ritualising and taming the Highlands. For the record, our beasts were mostly red with five brindles and five yellows – or more accurately golds.

After spaghetti and drams in the doorway of the Camusunary bothy I wandered over to check the boys before turning in. The rain, like my rage, had lifted and a young moon was scudding in and out of the clouds, dappling a gentle sea. I could hear Gavin bed-making for his dogs in an outhouse. In the bothy Julia was modelling and distributing outfits of navy-blue thermal underwear while George and Chris washed plates and JP tried his luck with the sad-looking girl.

The beasts had settled behind a crumbling stone dyke, their dark shapes looming large and prehistoric amidst the whitened tussocks. They had done well and I told them so. A juicy cudding and an apologetic cough were their only comments. On the shore the breakers swished and the shingle sighed.

It was a funny business this droving. Elation one minute, frustration the next and, with luck, contentment to follow. Drama, drollery and drudgery in equal parts. Like the fickle autumn light which in the Highlands changes by the hour, like the weather itself or the shy moon, we were in for dappled days, mixed fortunes. The bewildering speed with which hopes could be dashed or tempers lost would take some getting used to. Deprived of those habitual shelters – home and family, books and business, routine and reassurance – we felt hideously exposed. Like the boys we were at the mercy of unpredictable and elemental forces. Beasts used to the wilds of Knoydart and the indifference of Glen Coe were no doubt troubled by the unaccustomed and relentless scrutiny of men which droving involves. So our own sense of vulnerability was heightened by the awareness of being a focus of local attention. Alexander Smith's 'quickened sense of one's own identity' would last way beyond Glen Sligachan. With precious little else to which to nail one's colours, our masts of individuality assumed a rare and potentially ugly prominence. Not for nothing did Matilda, the individual *par excellence*, emerge as mascot.

6

'No' far away'

CAMUSUNARY TO LOCH SLAPIN

Our object in cutting through the Cuillins by way of Glen Sligachan had been threefold. We wanted to avoid having to follow the main road all the way to Broadford. We wanted somewhere to gain experience of cross-country droving in comparative seclusion. And we wanted to reach a sea loch on the south coast of the island called Loch Slapin. Poring over the map with a bit of knotted string I had calculated that Loch Slapin was almost exactly the same width as the crossing between Kylerhea and Glenelg. If we could persuade our boys to swim the comparatively placid waters of the loch it might be worth braving the much more dangerous currents of Kylerhea. Conversely, if beasts and drovers were going to get into difficulties they would stand a better chance of clambering ashore on the beaches of the loch than amidst the rocks of the kyle. Such, at least, was the theory. In the meantime Gavin and I had inspected the loch, approved its shoreline and made tentative arrangements for boats – boats, that is, for the drovers, not of course the cattle.

All cattle swim; big or small, black or red, it makes no difference. A story was currently going round Argyll of a cow that had just swum the Corryvreckan, the tidal whirlpool between the islands of Jura and Scarba. It climbed out on the other side and promptly gave birth to a fine calf. From South Uist came a letter with news of how even in this century (though, as the writer explained, 'a Uist twentieth century equals a Mull nineteenth century or a mainland eighteenth century') drovers used to swim their cattle as they island-hopped up to the Lochmaddy ferry on North Uist. 'And if it was neap tide they had a long way to swim. They [the drovers] stripped off their bottom half and hung on to the tail of a beast.' The MacGillivrays, Hugh and Ian, of Oban recalled stories of a great-uncle, Donald the Drover, who swam his beasts from Grasspoint on Mull to Kerrera or even direct to Oban, a distance of some five miles. Like many drovers Donald sent his dogs home as soon as he reached the tryst at Falkirk. They found their own way the hundred or so miles to Oban and then apparently swam unaccompanied back to Mull. This crossing would appear to be much the longest that was regularly swum by either dogs or cattle. Ian himself, when operating the Loch Etive ferry at Bonawe in the 1930s, had occasionally swum cattle and horses the three hundred yards to Achnacloich. He did not, however, pretend that it was easy. With a large herd you could take one on a rope behind the boat. 'The rest would follow. But you see, well, if they got round the bows, well they could upset the boat. Aye they could. Upset the boat.'

Like most of our informants he favoured tying the leader and working the rest from behind with a couple of small boats and the dogs. It seemed reasonable and received George's wholehearted approval. He would get a rope on the old girl – there was no question that Matilda was the leader – walk her into the water and then climb into a boat. She would swim alongside and the rest would follow – a resounding triumph for age and experience. It sounded wonderfully simple; with George so confident why should the rest of us, mere novices, be so apprehensive?

Besides, if it failed, there was an even simpler method well attested by an eighteenth-century witness. You simply drove the beasts down to the beach – 'they took to the water like spaniels' – and climbed into a boat behind them remembering all the while to utter 'a hideous cry'. 'This they [the drovers] told me they did to keep the foremost of them [the beasts]

from turning about; for in that case the rest would do likewise
and then they would be in danger to be driven away and
drowned by the current.' The witness omitted to include a
phonetic rendering of 'the hideous cry' but we all approved of
this dazzlingly easy solution and were prepared to scream,
yodel, howl and caterwaul for as long as it took to hit on the
magic formula.

Legging it over the ridge from Camusunary to Kilmarie in
the early morning I rehearsed a few tentative yelps. A herd of
cross shorthorns obligingly took to their heels. I tried it again.
Less obligingly they wheeled about and trotted back to in-
vestigate. Not a good omen.

Besides 'the roped leader' and 'the free swim', there was yet
one other possible approach. Infinitely more intimidating, this
third method was, for the Kylerhea crossing, much the best
authenticated, being sufficiently bizarre to have attracted the
attention of numerous writers. As early as the 1690s Dr Martin Martin, that connoisseur of the curious and the preternatu-
ral, had watched the drovers at Kylerhea with rapt attention.

> They begin when it is low water and fasten a twisted with about
> the lower jaw of each cow. The other end of the with is fastened to
> another cow's tail; and the number so tied together is commonly
> five. A boat with four oars rows off and a man sitting in the stern
> holds the with in his hand to keep up the foremost cow's head; and
> then all the five cows swim as fast as the boat rows; and in this way
> above a hundred may be ferried across in one day.

Dr Robertson, author of the Inverness agricultural survey,
provided further vital tips about this 'daisy chain' method. By
his day, 1813, ropes had mercifully replaced the confusing
'withs'.

> The drovers purchase ropes which are cut at a length of three feet
> having a noose at one end. This noose is put round the under jaw
> of each cow, taking care to have the tongue free. The reason given
> for having the tongue loose is that the animal may be able to keep
> the salt water from going down its throat in such a quantity as to
> fill all the cavities in the body which would prevent the action of
> the lungs; for every beast is found dead and said to be drowned at

3 Loch Slapin, Isle of Skye. The cattle swim but not across to the other side. Gavin tries to reason with them

4 Skye cattle leaving Kyleakin at the turn of the century

the landing place to which this mark of attention has not been paid. Whenever the noose is put under the jaw, all the beasts destined to be ferried together are led by the ferryman into the water until they are afloat, which puts an end to their resistance. Then every cow is tied to the tail of the cow before until a string of 6 or 8 be joined. A man in the stern of the boat holds the rope of the foremost cow. The rowers then ply their oars immediately.

The reason for these elaborate arrangements was obvious. Seen from the cliffs above, the kyle's six hundred yards of anguished water had looked bad enough. At shore level it looks infinitely worse. To the layman's eye the logic of two heavy Atlantic tides contesting a confined channel is belied by the reality of a squirming, surging chaos of urgent water with no two currents moving in the same direction. In flood, with the dominant tide gliding and slithering fast enough to smother the heaviest sea, it must be the most dangerous tidal strait in the British Isles. Even at slack water the currents can be treacherous. Allied to the fact that the only safe landing place for cattle was a small artificial slipway, this apparently precluded the possibility of any beasts swimming freely.

But did that mean we were stuck with 'the daisy chain'? Quite apart from the formidable difficulties and delays involved in roping each jaw and then, in the water, tying each tail, there was cause for strong reservations about the whole principle. The drove was controversial enough as it was. To those who queried whether it was right to expose the cattle to the stress and hardship of a two-hundred-mile trek we could – and did, repeatedly – emphasise that in the course of a day's grazing on the hill a Highlander may well cover as many miles as we would be driving them between stances; and that compared to the stress of a forty-ton transporter, droving was positively humane. We were inviting along the 'cruelty men' and we emphasised to both sponsors and critics that if at any point the beasts appeared to be suffering we would abandon the whole project. None of this was soft-talk. We were animal lovers all. If, with reasonable encouragement, the boys would swim, fine; but if not, if they had to be excessively manhandled into the water and forcibly dragged through it, we wanted no part in it. The most objectionable aspect of the 'daisy chain' was the idea of tying a beast to another's tail. Tails are sensitive, hard to tie and liable to come off. As early as 1800 there were those who thought such a practice 'abominably cruel', and so it is.

With the 'daisy chain' eliminated, our only hope of swimming the kyle was either to take each beast separately behind a boat or, flying in the face of tradition, to let most of them swim free and hope to contain and direct them with a veritable fleet of small craft. The more I thought about it the more relieved I was that we had allowed for trials on Loch Slapin.

At Kilmarie Mrs MacKinnon produced coffee and cream crackers while Ian, the factor for Strathaird Estate, volunteered to move his cross shorthorns; we could thus come straight down off the hill with a clear run to the sheltered field beside the main steading. It was typical of the kindness that was to last through the difficult days at Kilmarie. I sped back up the hill and at last found Gavin on top of the ridge. The beasts were just coming. Yes, they had taken four hours to do three miles; but I was not to jump to conclusions.

'Look, you think we've been farting about down there don't you? Morning coffee? Walking the dogs? Gin and tonics? Well let me tell you something. It's laminitis. Huh? Ever heard of laminitis, *bwana sahib*?'

Gavin is learning Swahili; as yet the results are not impressive. While I stall on the laminitis he produces half a loaf of wholemeal and a pound of orange cheese. A sandwich of sorts is constructed and washed down with a steaming, stimulant-free beverage supposedly made from barley. I suspect that even Gavin detests it; but he knows that if he filled his thermos, the only thermos, with tea or coffee he would be obliged to share it.

Laminitis, I now learn, is an inflammation inside the hoof,

peculiar to horses and ponies (not cattle, thank heavens) which causes lameness. Chris, the vet, this morning diagnosed it in Eilidh, the pretty bay pony. Julia and Gavin were detained in order to control the patient, leaving George to take the beasts off on his own. George, finding the loose boulders that pass for a road surface as uncongenial to cattle as they are to Land Rovers, attempted a direct ascent of the ridge. Three-quarters of the way up he got stuck with beasts unable to go left or right and unwilling to go up or down. He had waited – and slept – for an hour before dogs, ponies and drovers came to the rescue.

So much for the morning's happenings. In fact these prove to be only the loose end of a cord of causality stretching back to Sligachan and the night before last. According to the Buchanans, who reappear at Kilmarie, Eilidh is prone to laminitis. It seems to be induced by a diet too rich in protein. The hay and pony nuts can hardly be responsible but someone remembers that at Sligachan she managed to get her head in a sack of cattle cobs. Although I am still mystified how an incautious mouthful can produce lameness, all is now explained. In future more care will have to be taken to see that cattle and ponies are fed separately.

Gavin now produces an apple, and Brough and Chum, the two novice collies, suddenly jerk on their chains; Jody, the star of his troupe, merely faces about and pricks her ears. The beasts are coming. We turn to savour the spectacle.

The thrill and pride of watching the boys breasting a desolate horizon is something I cannot explain. It lasts throughout the drove and has lingered ever since. For the full effect one has to be in front and slightly below the level of the ridge. A backdrop of swirling cloud or, as in this case, of manicured and powdered peaks, helps. Pale and silky against the coarse black heather the cattle move with an aura of shaggy glory which defies the rugged scarps and gloomy corries. But this contrast is purely one of effect. The real message is again that sense of propriety, of things being as they should be, of beast and mountain complementing one another. I can never again relish the sight of Highlanders aimlessly chomping grass in a fenced paddock.

First over the top is one of the two large yellow bullocks. A hot contender for leadership of the drove, he is strongly fancied by Gavin who insists on calling him von Simpson; the reference, lost on us, is to 'someone I was at school with'. Von Simpson is followed by a tight bunch of his cronies all breathing heavily with heads lowered and horns swaying gently. It has been a hard push; in the cold air their breath is vapourising. Seconds later, but twenty yards to the left and apparently going in a different direction, two slight and flattened horns lurch into view. Beneath them a long rat's-tail fringe parts to reveal a wild and unmistakable eye. A cursing drover is in hot pursuit. Matilda gives him an angry look and testily turns back. From Gavin comes a bray of triumph. He suspects that behind my show of impartiality there lurks another Matilda man.

The whole ridge is now moving as the main van, followed by the ponies, breasts the skyline. This has been the highest and steepest climb they have to face on Skye. A halt is in order and we wander back to take a last look over Camusunary. Sunlight and showers are chasing one another across Gars Bheinn whilst, a few thousand feet below, the sea pounds at the base of the mountain. The view is perhaps the loveliest on Skye. To the south lies Rhum and in the foreground Soay, low and deserted. But it is the Cuillins packing the horizon from west to north that command attention. 'The hills seemed to possess some secret, to brood over some unutterable idea which you can never know,' wrote Alexander Smith, the spasmodic poet, 'you are impressed with the notion that the mountains are silent because they are listening so intently.'

Beneath this forbidding spectacle Camusunary ('the bay-of-the-shieling') nestles in pastoral serenity, an island of green between the black-and-tan of heather and bracken and the grey churning sea. A small dark figure that must be JP is loading the Land Rover on the beach by the bothy. The only other building, a smart and empty whitewashed cottage, momentarily basks in a shaft of sunlight. I understand now why Gavin was raving about the place. He once spent a summer as gillie on the small river which dashes into the sea at the far end of the beach. Gillie at Camusunary – one could do worse. A clack of horns jolts us back to reality. Most of the cattle are resting or quietly grazing but two brindle beasts have decided to fight. It does not look serious and soon becomes recognised as part of the normal pattern. Well matched in terms of bulk and colouring these two are destined to devote every spare minute to sparring. The result is, and will remain, inconclusive because one has up-turning horns and the other is a down-turn. We have three or four down-turns, their horns arcing towards the muzzle as on a Hereford bull though much wider. I have read somewhere that they are the 'kindlier feeders' and it is certainly no stigma. But when such horns meet with the more conventional flat and slightly upturning horns they lock neatly together. Nose to nose Upturn Brindle and Downturn Brindle spend happy hours pushing and shoving in this pointless clinch. None of the other beasts pays a blind bit of attention; soon neither do we. It is just a useful indicator that all is well.

The ponies race on ahead and we plunge down after them heading for hedgerows, green fields and civilisation. In exemplary order we enter a gate in the deer fence and trundle across the hill park. The river at the bottom is in spate. Sensing that the day's work is already over the boys breast the current without a murmur. They edge diagonally across and scramble up the bank streaming with water. Tonight they have a field to themselves with shelter and water; and the drovers have a cottage.

Strathaird is MacKinnon country. That evening, in search of swimming lore, we descended on the nearby village of Elgol to quiz a MacKinnon who had supposedly swum beasts from

Soay. In so small a place the address seemed irrelevant until, after half a dozen false trails, the right MacKinnon still eluded us. It was like asking for Singh in Southall. Half the population were MacKinnons.

Kilmarie, the big house, was built by one of the more fastidious of the clan. He first erected his baronial mansion on the lochside but 'finding the air hard to breathe' caused it to be removed to a site well back and above the road. This time the air was fine. But the view was not; it was too far from the loch. The place was abandoned and remains so. Meanwhile, a few critical yards from the mouth of the river, a site was found which was just right, Kilmarie.

The house, and the estate, are now the property of Ian Anderson otherwise Jethro Tull, musician. He was on tour at the time and I never discovered whether Tull, the musician and laird, was consciously imitating Tull, the eighteenth-century English agriculturalist. He has certainly made some improvements. Receipts and royalties from the music business have been ploughed, fenced and stocked into the estate on a lavish scale. The tractors are new, the grass lush, and the cattle grazing it include the only herd of Highlanders now to be found on Skye. The factor insisted that they were kept not as a rich man's indulgence but because they were the most efficient feeders on marginal ground. Our own observations of their passion for heather and bog myrtle rather bore this out.

The cottage was in keeping with the general air of optimism. It was newly converted, furnished from a Habitat catalogue and spotless. It was not what drovers were used to and we tripped across the fitted carpet and gunned the hot-water system with a delicious sense of guilt. Even drovers can strike lucky.

Two miles up the road lived Robert Kelly, Tull's right-hand man first as road manager and latterly as salmon farm manager. Like the MacKinnons – all of them – the Kellys combined hospitality with help and encouragement. Their big new bungalow stands on a spit of land between the salmon cages and the loch at a place called Faoilean ('the sand-bank'). It was here that we had chosen for the swim.

* * *

'Bloody hopeless. If we could just get one to keep going the rest might get the idea. But if the first beasts keep buggering about there's no way the others can get out there.'

Reservations about swimming the cattle were proving pitifully inadequate. Soaked to the armpits, blue with cold, and mad with frustration we were getting nowhere.

'Aye, but see John, if Charlie there had come in behind and one of us had jumped in with him, well, they'd go. Aye, they'd go. I think they'd go. We'll give them a rest. See what I mean? Who's for a drop of the cratur now?'

George was still optimistic but his confidence had taken a terrible hammering. As a first ploy we had rigged up a funnel of ropes and stobs to channel the beasts into the water. It looked pretty ineffectual and it was; it was cosmetic. With Matilda on a halter George proudly tugged her on stage like a reluctant competitor in the local dog show. We massed the rest of the beasts behind and briefly it must have looked like a well-orchestrated operation. Things started to go wrong as soon as Matilda discovered that the steeply shelving beach was composed of large loose pebbles. We had forgotten her phobia for such things and now paid the price. All forward momentum was lost as we rushed to George's aid. Shoved and practically lifted into the water, Matilda still fretted over the footing and when eventually a rope attached to her halter was thrown to Chris in the boat, I think she swam simply to get off the stones.

The boat, a sturdy affair usually used to ferry tourists to Loch Coruisk, proceeded to chug up and down twenty yards off-shore with Matilda wallowing at the end of the long line like an angler's nightmare. All that remained was to convince twenty-seven bullocks that she was having a marvellous time. With menacing sticks and cries as hideous as we could make them, drovers advanced, beasts surged forwards and miscellaneous onlookers closed in behind. We crashed down the shingle and entered the water. There we stopped. The noise increased, sticks flew, tempers flared and the beasts scarcely budged. They swam all right and every time a tightly packed flotilla struck out for the open water we thought we had it. Then they turned. They wanted to come back.

'Too tame,' muttered a MacKinnon in a deer-stalker, 'it's wilder beasts you'll be needing.'

Anticipating this homing instinct we had devised a masterly strategy which involved Robert Kelly, the 'roadie', patrolling one flank in an inflatable (admittedly not the preferred craft for engaging horned cattle) and Charlie MacKinnon, a wise and resourceful local with a fibreglass rowing boat, patrolling the other. As the beasts turned yet again, those on shore were understandably less inclined to admire the skills of the boatmen or to appreciate the beauty of the strategy. Actually both worked well – in fact too well. Spying the flashing oars of Charlie or Robert's vicious little outboard the beasts forwent any idea of outflanking and preferred to swim straight back into their advancing comrades. Anyone familiar with rush hour on the London Underground will appreciate the disappointing result. Horn smacked against horn as, unable to elbow through, those on their way back deflected the others and were themselves deflected until a whirlpool effect was achieved. Should a drover charge in to try and break it up, either the beasts struck out for the gap thus left in the shore defences or the drover was sucked into the vortex at the mercy of fifty-four long and lethal horns.

It was at about this point that an interesting statistic came to light. Of the six intrepid drovers only two, Julia and JP, were swimmers. (Possibly Chris too only he was still out on the loch playing Matilda; I myself was learning.) It was not actually necessary to swim; in fact the water was so full of hairy backs and handy horns that it was scarcely possible. But the discovery, I felt, immeasurably damaged our whole moral position. We could keep it quiet and indeed did so. But it sapped at our resolve, and the beasts, to whom the whiff of a psychological advantage was as exciting as a roadside vegetable patch, proceeded to exploit it unmercifully. They knew that in deep water they could confidently call our bluff.

By now Matilda was listing heavily and appeared to be in some distress. Had Chris been a fisherman he would have been reeling in and reaching for the gaff. Instead he released the rope and, like the one that got away, she lurched back to life and paddled vigorously ashore. In spite of bringing half the loch with her, she skipped across the pebbles with suspicious ease. She had done her job and now positioned herself to enjoy the spectacle.

For what was to be the final sally of the day there were nearly as many drovers as cattle. The clan MacKinnon, who had so far refrained from interfering other than by offering polite and pithy advice – mostly in Gaelic – now armed themselves with long bamboo staves and joined in the fray. A mob of children – amongst whom I recognised my own – provided back-up. Again we crashed across the shingle and into the icy water. This time the hideous cries were bilingual. If there is anything in the theory that Highland cattle only understand Gaelic they should have responded. In fact, like well-rehearsed actors, they turned in an identical performance – the hopeful surge into open water, the hesitation, the turn, the mêlée, and the whirlpool. Dangling from a broad hairy back to catch my breath I glimpsed the opposite shore, now receding to an impossible distance, and above it a conical mountain of startling symmetry. Match this, it seemed to be saying; you expect to march in here and turn a herd of Highlanders into a circus act? Forget it.

Suitably chastened we gathered up the beasts and prepared for the two-mile squelch back to Kilmarie. The tide had turned – not that it made much difference if we were never to get more than a few yards into the water – pneumonia threatened, and the MacKinnons had crofts to attend to. Round One to the beasts.

★   ★   ★

Round Two was next day and about half a mile further up the loch. Instead of the steep shingle beach we selected a shallower spot with a sandy bottom where the tide probed the grassy foreshore in irregular crenellations. There was a lot of seaweed and the loch was in fact wider here. But it was slightly more sheltered, an important consideration with the wind distinctly keener and the water as cold as ever.

The other significant innovation was that we brought only eleven beasts. On the previous afternoon all the boys had been put through the handling pens at Kilmarie. Those who, because of the spread of their horns, had been unable to enter the 'race' at Oban mart had been subjected to the magnesium bullet and a squirt of worm dose. In the process Goldie, a rather effeminate-looking creature with a silky fringe of outrageous proportions, was set aside for observation – another possible case of transit fever/pneumonia. And at the same time a dab of red paint was daubed on those unfortunate enough to be selected for the first XI.

The idea was simply to reduce the drove to manageable proportions for what we now all acknowledged as experimental work rather than proving trials. The smaller beasts had shown little relish for the water and they had invariably got in the way on those critical occasions when a close follow-up of the leading swimmers might have kept them on course. It was an admission of defeat, but better to swim eleven than none.

With bursts of sunshine adding zest but no warmth to the scene a small covey of photographers followed us down to the shore. The BBC's television crew would have shown up had it been midnight. We would have preferred to see this one through off-camera and they rightly suspected as much. It isn't easy to give the slip to a producer hungry for action when you are encumbered with a herd of cattle. But at least he sensed stern business in prospect and settled for the telephoto. To the reporter/presenter went the unenviable job of interviewing, or distracting, the man from the SPCA.

Instead of piling on the waterproofs today I peeled them off. A shirt, threadbare jeans and delapidated tennis shoes would suffice; a wet suit would have been better still. JP in typically inconspicuous fashion had, I noticed, also stripped. It was a measure of our commitment. We dispensed with the ropes and the stage-management and got down to business.

Like the party-giver anxious to get things going with a swing we opened with a full-blooded assault devoid of frills and subtlety. Voices still hoarse from yesterday roared into life as we waded through the weed. When the water reached rib level I realised that the beasts must be well and truly afloat. The leaders were twenty yards out and Charlie was rowing round behind to take over the momentum. In a reasonable depth of water the beasts were actually easier to handle than on shore. To some extent you could even direct them by administering a mighty shove from behind or by steering their horns. I was so delighted by this discovery that I missed the fatal moment when the leaders noticed that Charlie had come round behind and that his flank was therefore unguarded. They came ashore a stone's throw up the loch and stood there streaming water and eyeing us reproachfully.

Julia chucked a brimming wellington at them in disgust.

'Maybe that man was right. I mean look at them. They wouldn't even make off cross country let alone across the loch. They're too damn tame, think it's some sort of game.'

All right, well we would show them, cruelty man or no cruelty man. Back in the water George and Gavin got a rope on one of the larger beasts and Chris hauled him alongside the boat. They chugged gently and temptingly away as we hurled ourselves at the remaining ten. When a beast glanced back it was no longer a question of waving a stick. You charged straight in. We could have got a herd of kangaroos treading water if it was all down to commitment. In particular JP was like a man possessed. Hitherto he had given the cattle a wide berth, happy to leave their welfare in the hands of those whose livelihood depended on understanding animals. But the crisis produces the hero. He was launching himself to left and right like a frenetic scrum-half. Gone was the philosopher's pensive image as he emitted an unbroken stream of oaths. At one point he passed clean over the beast I was piloting and locked onto the horns of a nonplussed von Simpson. Three thousand years ago he would have been a sensation at Knossos.

Alas, there was to be no sensation on Loch Slapin. We redeployed, we cut out five beasts at a time, we experimented with a noose round the lower jaw, we tried everything. The boat slowly edged into the middle of the loch. None would follow. Round Two to the beasts.

As I collapsed on the grass, benumbed fingers groping for a dram, the BBC cornered me for an interview.

'Give it plenty of fire this time,' said the producer, 'you tend to underplay it.'

Plenty of fire? I was indigo with cold – it could, I suppose, have been the dye off my shirt – and my teeth were chattering so fiercely I was afraid of biting the bottle. A more abject, gibbering figure of failure never appeared on screen. Even as I pointed across the loch at our one modest triumph still bobbing alongside the boat there was a panicky revving of the engine. According to Chris the beast had abruptly stopped swimming. Taking no chances he ordered the full ahead. In the event it was fine. It swam ashore into the open arms of Julia who had driven round the loch and half an hour later it was back with its companions none the worse for the experience.

Looking back I am sure that we did nothing wrong. Wilder cattle might indeed have been less inclined to return to their tormentors. But on dry land such wild beasts would have been more than inexperienced drovers could cope with and anyway, given the nature of droving, they would not have remained wild for long. Our beasts were not at this stage particularly tame but a week or two later, when drovers and cattle were each more confident of the other, I think we might have made it. They certainly waded burns and swam rivers without objection.

Of course, we became more canny. We knew the leaders (and, more important, so did they) and we would simply concentrate on getting two or three of these across. The rest would follow with minimal encouragement. In the old days at recognised crossings like Inverbeg on Loch Lomond the local inn kept a couple of experienced beasts solely to act as pilots to lead the droves across the loch. Whether there was ever any such arrangement at Kylerhea is not recorded but there would certainly have been cattle on both sides of the water. The presence, and above all the noise, of the cattle on the opposite shore would have constituted a powerful stimulus to bovine curiosity. Someone had actually suggested we take a cow with calf specifically for this purpose. The idea was that you transported the calf across by boat and left it to call for its mother on the other side. I could see this working well but I doubt if the cruelty man would have approved.

We could perhaps have tried taking a few beasts round to the other side, but would they at this stage have missed their companions sufficiently to summon them across the water? The trouble was that the cohesion of the drove was as yet too fragile. An intricate and binding pattern of relationships was slowly being forged between beast and beast. It was fascinating to watch but on Day Five the process was still far from complete.

Something similar could be said of the drovers. That evening round a pine and polyurethane table amidst the louvres and the pretty cotton prints of our Habitat cottage we faced the first real crisis of confidence. Each of us had his own reasons for being here but all of us were also in it for the fun – or the hell – of it, whichever the case might be. But did that have to include being made a fool of? I was inclined to think yes but those with a standing in the agricultural world could hardly be expected to agree.

Specifically, what did we do now? In the next-door cottage the BBC were piling on the pressure. They badly needed the swim at Kylerhea. The programme editor was back-tracking and only the spectacle of thirty beasts bobbing across to the mainland would guarantee his continued commitment to the project. I took this threat seriously not because the television coverage was doing anything for the drove but because the main sponsors – Famous Grouse Whisky, Scottish Agricultural Industries and Land Rover – had certain expectations. To their credit none of them attempted to sway the issue one way or the other. But with no further prospect of the camera occasionally brushing past their products they could reasonably have left us to fend for ourselves without cattle feed, whisky, or the means to transport them.

Outside the cottage the case for the defence was represented by a small blue van patrolling the Broadford road under an angry sky. John Grundy, the Skye officer of the SPCA, was not an unreasonable man. He had found nothing reprehensible about the antics on Loch Slapin and though deeply concerned about what might transpire at Kylerhea he had not yet registered implacable opposition. Another day of trials on the loch might change everything and this, to George's way of thinking, was the only sensible course.

'Ach, we're no far away, I'm telling you. If . . . Well, if . . . Well, you know yourself, if . . . Aye, they'll go. I'm telling you.'

George had always maintained that swimming cattle was as natural as nuts in May. We were ever on the brink of success needing the merest nudge of luck or inspiration. But tonight, as the first blast of the next gale rattled the sashes, George sensed that for once we were unconvinced by the voice of experience. Much in Chris's mind was the beast who had stopped swimming half way across the loch. Gavin was embarrassed about making any more demands of the MacKinnons and I was painfully aware that morale could hardly stand another day of defeats. We would leave for Broadford in the morning. The swimming was over.

George, like Captain Oates, made for the door and, muttering something about sleeping with the beasts, disappeared into the gale. JP went with him, more as chaperone than sympathiser.

7

'That rude primeval traffic'

LOCH SLAPIN TO BROADFORD AND KYLERHEA

George still contends that with another day on Loch Slapin the beasts would have swum it.

'If we'd put the cattle in the water that Saturday morning, they'd the wind behind them. They'd have gone right across. Aye, with the wind behind them. That's my opinion.'

To connoisseurs – and by now we undoubtedly qualified as such – the gale of October 10th was exceptional. Rounding the head of the loch I went hand over hand along the railings of the bridge to keep myself from being blown off. The tents in which JP and George had slept collapsed themselves during breakfast and when, later in the day, Gavin chose to experiment with a golf umbrella it took just two minutes for the wind to shred it and snatch away every vestige of material.

Each gust brought something different in the way of precipitation. Dashing in and out of the loch through sleet, hail and torrential rain would have been suicidal. And if the beasts *had* shown a preference for the water and if they *had* then been blown across, it would have proved nothing. At Kylerhea the tides were critical enough; with the added complication of having to wait for a favourable gale we might have been there all winter.

'Good luck, boys.' An elderly lady doled out biscuits from the shelter of her doorway as we were blown through Torrin. From the butcher George returned triumphant with a bloody bundle of liver and kidneys. It was our first village but there were few faces. As the butcher explained, it was the wildest twenty-four hours anyone could remember.

The road, a single track between high hedges, snaked between the crofts and then emerged into open country beside the reedy waters of Loch Cill Chriosd. A forlorn graveyard with a few twisted rowans and a well-cropped sward cried out for the sketchpad, whilst at a respectful distance conical mountains of improbable symmetry dotted the rolling landscape. These are the Red Hills, the granite counterparts of the gabbro Cuillins. Whereas time has chiselled the gabbro into a set of flashy dentures, jagged and sheer, here it has patiently sanded the granite to produce hills so neatly contoured that on the map they look like targets. In profile a whiff of smoke at the apex would suggest volcanoes; but the eye is sadly prejudiced by the recollection of slag heaps.

In the afternoon the wind slackened and veered behind us. By the time the Bay of Broadford opened ahead, it was a gentle drying breeze stroking the sedges of a now calm and smiling heath. Apart from some embarrassing forays into the crofts of Torrin the beasts had behaved admirably. They filed along in two ranks, one each side of the tarmac. From behind one looked over and along a column of red backs interspersed with horns that dipped rhythmically. Sometimes the horns seemed not to be moving at all, just the shoulders and haunches gently rolling. The effect was hypnotic.

'Reckon the salt water's done them a power of good. Kills off the keds and any skin infections.' Chris at least was his usual placid self. He spoke of the dying keds with the relish of a pest controller. It was consoling to learn that out of two days of sheer hell some good had come.

Now that he mentioned it the boys were indeed looking rather fine. Submersed in the sea and dry-blown by the gale their coats had acquired what hairdressers call 'lift'. The pile ruffled in the breeze; even Matilda's improbable conformation was decently disguised. When the sinking sun threw a dazzling shaft straight at us, the pile took fire, outlining each beast in a shaggy blur of flame. From feathered feet to bleached forelocks they blazed in glory. Their horns, honed and polished by the glare, were born aloft as trophies. Watching them was like seeing a vision. A crowd of birch saplings bowed beside the road. I swear there was music.

How pathetically inadequate is the film camera. Here were we, ten feet tall, treading glory and breasting the last rise before Broadford to the strains of Beethoven's Fifth, while all the camera could convey was a herd of brown cows straggling along the A881 with two or three scruffy herdsmen staring dumbly into space. The film-makers wanted action. They would dub a bit of William Tell over the swimming trials and they were looking forward to a Celtic version of Pamplona through the thoroughfares of Broadford. Cattle droving has, I suppose, got that image. Nothing could be further from the reality.

Of course, even as one tried to formulate the simple majesty of it all, the scene fell apart in an embarrassing outburst of activity. The beasts had got wind of some hill cattle down by the Broadford river. We too had seen them. They were half a mile away and mooing provocatively. Our boys mooed back but appeared to be resisting the temptation of a closer acquaintance. Seconds later we could no longer hold them; they were gone, high-tailing it round the hill and taking the opposition by surprise with a rollicking charge. For beasts that had already walked some seven miles they lacked neither wind nor pace. This was more than could be said of Chris and me. By the time we reached the top of the hill the rout was continuing on the far side of the river and heading for the Cuillins.

It was all down to Jody now. Gavin, who as usual was out in front lending tone to the procession, slipped her leash and she shot off for the river. Somewhere in the dead ground beyond she turned the combined herd and in ten minutes she was back pushing along fifty head of assorted cattle and hugely pleased at having so easily augmented our stock. I sneaked her a bit of chocolate. In return she graciously assisted in shedding the strangers. It had been a classic performance and convincing testimony of the value of dogs.

*   *   *

In Broadford George Campbell, licensee of the Broadford
Hotel, waited to take us under his wing. 'Since the Broadford
Hotel was originally a droving inn', he had written, 'we should
be delighted to offer hospitality to the drovers if they should
care to fit a "refreshment halt" into their schedule. If the aim
is to re-create a highland drove of old, then a halt at Broadford
is unavoidable.' This was both generous and accurate. As
regular travellers and thirsty talkers the drovers who came to
Skye in search of livestock were always popular with the
innkeepers. In 1837 Joseph Mitchell, the road engineer, found
the inn at Sconser near Sligachan packed with drovers. Even
at the breakfast table – 'Salmon, cod, mackerel, fowls, beef and
potatoes etc.' – there was much 'higgling' over cattle prices.

> 'Och, ye're a hard man, Greshornish, I canna think of geeing you
> ony such price. It winna afeurd it. God bless you, mon, ye hae no
> notion hoo prices are doon i' the south. Just tak the money offered
> and let's make a bargain at yeance.'
> 'No, confound you, MacFarlane, you are offering for the stots
> when I know you are for the cows also, so you better say £3 15s for
> the whole over head.'

It was September 20th, the second day of the great cattle fair
at Sligachan, held on the spot where we had had our first
stance. Soon after Mitchell's visit a hotel was built there, no
doubt to cash in on the fair. By the 1880s it was a place of
grand repute with a varied and exotic clientele – 'everyone
from tourists, travellers, members of the Alpine Club, distinguished artists, statesmen, ecclesiastics, botanists, geologists,
yachting parties, pleasure-seekers of all sorts, drovers, excisemen, right down to that class of tourist who "does" Skye as a
sort of unpleasant duty'. In such company the drovers were
almost as unpopular as the excisemen. Traveller after traveller
complained of their rowdiness and took exception to their
tobacco smoke. A drover, left to tackle his plum duff with a
dainty dessert spoon, was heard to bellow across the dining

room for the return of his soup spoon. 'Hoots, lassie, isna ma mouth just as big for pudding as for kail?' We, like him, were no doubt an embarrassment; I trust, though, good for trade.

The drover who put up at an inn was commonly 'from the south country', which might be anywhere from Lochaber down to Stirling. Although it could not be said that any particular clan made droving their speciality, many seem to have been descendants of the MacFarlanes and MacGregors whose cattle lifting had so disrupted trade in the skirts of the Highlands (especially Dunbartonshire and Perthshire) during the early eighteenth century. Now, in the nineteenth century, they might be men of some substance, forerunners of our Oban patron, Hughie. Those who purchased their cattle outright might be carrying £500 in their pocket books and have spent the lot before the fair was over. Others paid by promissory notes and some seem to have operated on a commission basis; there was no standard practice in such matters. But, for all, the commitment was considerable and, whatever the financial arrangements, the drover/dealer – who was often also the topsman in charge of the drove – was a man to be reckoned with. Even today Gaelic speakers in the Hebrides use the word 'drobhair' to refer to dealers from the mainland, like Hughie, rather than to the actual stockmen.

The difference between the drover/dealer with his wad of notes, his pony and his fast talk, and the herdsman/stockman who actually tended the cattle was one of age and means. 'Sixpence a day', explained a bent old man leaning on a bent old gate in Broadford. 'Aye, sixpence a day, that was it. There was the five shillings before we left and there was the five shillings I brought back.' He might have been in his eighties and was probably no more than ten or twelve when he joined a drove; young boys were reckoned the best of herdsmen. That still made it no earlier than 1905 and I wish there had been time to hear more of his story. These were the lads whose departure from hearth and home occasioned such heart-rending scenes and whose return to the glen was often awaited

in vain. On sixpence a day they did not stay in hotels. At the
Sligachan Fair Mitchell noted that both crofters and drovers
were also sleeping rough with their cattle.

> The whole aspect of the place – a bare and barren mountainside –
> was wild and savage. It had been raining all night and as most of
> the people had been either up drinking or sleeping on the bare
> ground during the night, they had a dirty and dishevelled appear-
> ance. The gentlemen had a blowsy and unshaven aspect, the
> horses were ungroomed and, there being no stables, little gillies
> [i.e. drovers' lads] with kilts, bare heads and bare legs were
> mounted and with much glee were riding backwards and forwards
> along the road . . . [Others were] leaning on their sticks or lying
> on the damp ground, their faithful collies at their feet panting for
> employment. Such was the fair at Sligachan which I viewed with
> no very favourable impression of the civilisation of the people.

There were three such fairs on Skye – Portree, Sligachan
and Broadford. Some twenty years before Mitchell's visit, that
of Dr John MacCulloch coincided with the Portree fair. He
described his hotel as 'a parliament of drovers . . . and all the
town began to look like a stable'. After so much talk of bone
and breed, pedigree and prices, MacCulloch told Sir Walter
Scott that he might buy and sell a stot himself 'purely out of
respect for the dignity and antiquity of this ancient science'.

The Broadford fair was held about a mile outside the town
at a spot still marked as 'Market Stance' on the Ordnance
Survey map. On the ground it is less obvious. With the idea
that it might be suitable for an overnight stance we had paced
about in the bog and heather but found nothing to recommend
it over any other acre of the surrounding moor. You could see
the place from above the field where our pneumonia patient
and his companion had spent the last few days and where they
were now joined by the rest of the drove. As in Glen Drynoch
it was impossible to imagine such a desolate location ever
having been a scene of great animation.

Yet, according to Alexander Smith, our spasmodic poet, for
the fair both sides of the road for fully a mile were lined with
rows of cattle, 'the wildest looking creatures with fells of hair

dangling over their eyes and tossing horns of preposterous dimensions'. There were flocks of sheep 'with insane dogs and men flying along their edges' and on every knoll women in white bonnets and scarlet plaids sat apart with their solitary cows staked beside them. In the hollows tents had been set up, rough constructions of hazel sticks and blankets, at which boiled potatoes and Talisker drams were on offer. Here the drovers – 'rough-looking customers enough' – thronged in a haze of pipe smoke and steaming tweed. Smith was more taken by a gayer congregation of 'fair-haired and scarlet-plaided girls' who swarmed round another set of booths at which sweets, ribbons and cheap jewellery were the attraction. The fair was an immense social occasion, 'the Skye-man's exchange, his family gathering and his newspaper'. 'It was a strange sight that rude primeval traffic.'

Such fairs, or markets, were held throughout the Highlands and Islands from as early as May through till November. There is a list of some five hundred but many were small *ad hoc* affairs with the drovers simply arriving on the scene and letting it be known that they were in the market for beasts. Others were not specifically cattle fairs; there were fairs for horses and ponies and fairs of a purely retail character at which packmen and peddlers set up their stalls. But the three fairs of Skye may be taken as typical of their kind; it was at such gatherings that the droves were made up and it was from them that men and beasts started the long journeys by which they would all eventually converge on the great Lowland markets of, principally, Crieff and later Falkirk.

Droves setting off from the Broadford fair immediately joined the throng of beasts coming from the rest of Skye. All had to pass through Broadford, those from Sleat and Loch Eishort as well as those from Elgol, Strathaird and Torrin, here joining the main van from the north of the island and from the west coast. We too, after a week's initiation in the Cuillins and on the shores of Loch Slapin, would now make straight for the mainland along what was once the high road to Crieff.

*   *   *

The high road to Crieff is of course a misnomer. Drove roads now being drove roads in no more than name it had been necessary to heed the solicitor's advice 'to obtain the formal consent of all owners of land over which you propose to drive the cattle'. This, I had imagined, meant mailing out a standard letter with our imposing letterhead inviting all concerned to give their permission. I passed it over to Julia as the better typist; besides lairds would respond more favourably to the feminine approach.

'Yes, but who am I supposed to send this to?'

'Just make a list and tick them off as you go. You know, Forestry Commission, um, Black Mount Estate, er, Lochiel.'

'That's three.'

'Well, phone round. Must be a directory of landowners.'

Three weeks later the list had about eight names and three-quarters of the route was still unaccounted for. How *did* one discover to whom a particular chunk of mountain, an inviting little track, belonged? Who, in fact, owns the Highlands? Left-wing pamphlets which purported to answer this question and, in the process, to reveal the iniquities of private landownership, proved unhelpful. Their information was either out of date or not specific enough. There were no obvious directories and though door-to-door enquiries (with fifteen miles between each door) revealed some tenants and factors they left the actual proprietors as mysterious as ever.

This problem was eventually solved by the officials of the Department of Agriculture and Fisheries for Scotland (DAFS), and by Colonel Sir Donald Cameron of Lochiel KT CVO. The former produced maps, beautiful sepia and rose sheets at about six inches to the mile, which marked every crag and corrie and on which the boundaries of the various farms and estates had all been neatly drawn. The DAFS were also, it transpired, proprietors in their own right, especially of crofting ground and small farms. On Skye the Department is

actually the largest landowner. Rightly we – or rather Julia –
had still to approach each tenant-farmer or the clerk of each
crofting township; but armed with a list of names and addres-
ses and writing with the blessing of the Department she forged
confidently ahead. The list suddenly grew to three pages.

To Sir Donald Cameron, or Lochiel, we were indebted for
the discovery of SLoF. (Many lairds and clan chiefs are still
known by the name of their estate; most welcome the practice;
some, like the laird of Muck, do not.) Lochiel's estate be-
strode our preferred route's entrance to the Great Glen (the
diagonal fault between Fort William and Inverness). I knew
this and knowing that he was also connected with the Highland Cattle Society I had placed great store by winning his
support. First approaches were not encouraging. Evidently
some process of consultation was going on amongst the Highland lairds. The signs were ominous. Late-night phone calls
hinted darkly at a clan revolt. They were worried about possible damage to fences and forestry; they didn't want us messing
up the stalking; and who were we anyway? Not knowing
whence these sinister rumours emanated we were powerless to
combat them.

Then came a letter from SLoF, the Scottish Landowners
Federation, a body so august that you know of it only if you
belong to it. The letter referred to the correspondence with
Lochiel and voiced misgivings. Julia replied with reassur-
ances. A few days later at six in the morning I was on my way
to Inverness; the SLoF was meeting, the drove was on the
agenda, and it was just possible that a personal appearance
might tip the balance.

The venue was a boardroom at the back of the Eden Court
Theatre. My nearest-thing-to-a-city-suit was obviously appropriate and an assurance that I would not run on into the lunch
break went down well. Far from being sinister, SLoF seemed
rather genial. Their main objection was that a herd of cattle
crossing the high passes with dogs, ponies and drovers was
going to create havoc amongst the stags at a time when the

stalking season was at its height. In Wester Ross and Inverness-shire we would be entering some of the choicest glens. Sportsmen, mainly from Germany and the Low Countries, pay hefty fees for a blitzkrieg against the red deer and no estate can afford the embarrassment of any untoward disturbance. In the last weeks of September, when we would have expected to be crossing this area, the rut, or mating season, would be about to begin. The antlers of the stags, having grown to their maximum extent and having shed their velvet covering, are then at their majestic peak. So too is the condition of the meat, but during the rut the stags neglect their regular habits and soon become out of condition. There is thus only a brief and critical period when the trophy-bagging interests of the sportsmen and the venison-marketing interests of the estates coincide.

But September was also the critical month for droving. How they resolved this conflict of interests a century ago is not clear. Professor Haldane has suggested that the decline of droving had as much to do with attempts to confine the drovers to roads and to charge them for grazing as it did with the coming of the railways. If this was so, it seems probable that in the Highlands the stalking lobby was the main culprit. The growing popularity of sheep as opposed to cattle during the nineteenth century would certainly account for a drop in numbers. But passing droves would not exactly have stripped the hillsides. On the contrary, if anything they improved the grazing, cattle being less choosy in their feeding than sheep and more generous with their manuring. If landowners were behind the attempts to confine droving to the new roads it seems much more probable that they had realised that droving was incompatible not with sheep farming but with those few critical weeks of stalking. It can also be no coincidence that after 1833, 'the first year [according to a contemporary] that the Highlands became the rage and that deer forests were made and rented', droving declined as steadily as sporting interests prospered.

Sporting interests, now respectable by virtue of their earn-
ing good Guilders and Deutschmarks, are still paramount. We
needed SLoF rather more than they needed us; we would have
to fit in. When I suggested that we could postpone the drove
by a month a murmur of approval passed round the mahogany
table. We would still just coincide with the stag shooting; the
season does not officially end until October 21st. But during
the last two weeks the rut is in full roar and the stags are wary.
Most estates would expect to have shot whatever the Red Deer
Commission had decreed as their complement by the end of
the first week in October.

It seemed a reasonable concession at the time. The alternative, to have brought the drove forward a month, would have
invited all sorts of problems – roads choked with tourist
traffic, cattle exhausted by the heat, and drovers demented by
the midges (or, in Gaelic apparently – and much more aptly –
the 'meaniehulagans'). The only obvious disadvantage of
October lay in the shorter daylight hours. At the time this
appeared a matter of little consequence and I wondered that
the drovers of old had not simply delayed their operations.

Having pledged its support, SLoF swung behind the drove
with gusto. One list of relevant landowners came from its
Inverness branch and another from Perth. Julia was onto her
fifth sheet of foolscap. Some owners, or syndicates, preferred
to preserve their anonymity behind the address of a solicitor;
permission came but we never knew where from. There was a
Spanish marquesa who never replied and a Belgian count who
had forgotten to leave a forwarding address. Some estates were
changing hands so fast we never caught up with the current
owners. The largest extent of ground we had to cross was
owned not, as expected, by the Forestry Commission, but by
British Aluminium. There were tobacco barons, merchant
bankers and Oxford dons. There were also hard-pressed farmers, nervous hoteliers and ultra-polite crofters. With just one
exception, none refused their permission and many offered a
field for the beasts, a campsite for the drovers and sometimes

even accommodation. Such an enthusiastic response was beyond all expectations. It felt good to be living in the Highlands.

The one exception was a crofter, said to be English and originally from Essex, who lived at Kylerhea. Although permission had been forthcoming from the owner of the land, the Dagenham Crofter made it plain that he had studied his rights and had no intention of co-operating. Kylerhea consists of about a dozen whitewashed croft houses dotted about a verdant hollow between the mountains and the sea at the bottom of a steep glen. All except three of the houses are usually empty, the Dagenham Crofter's only neighbours being a charming but elderly lady and Terry Nutkins, a television personality who presents wild-life programmes for children. The BBC were therefore frequent visitors to Kylerhea and our antagonist perhaps resented this. It is the only explanation that makes any sense.

*   *   *

On Sunday, the seventh day, the drove rested in a field on the outskirts of Broadford. Sunday droving had always been a contentious issue. The ministers condemned it and as often as not the drovers ignored the injunction. Such at least was the situation on the mainland. But in the Islands it seems unlikely that anyone ever moved cattle on the Sabbath. Observing the Lord's Day was, and is, a Hebridean prerogative. To George our willingness to observe local custom in the matter was so crucial that, along with unlimited dry socks, he had made it a precondition of his joining the drove. With an ambivalence not untypical of the Islands he and Chris chose to spend the day combing Broadford's bars in search of the most convivial. JP retired to the hills to read about Zen and the Art of Motorcycle Maintenance; Gavin gathered up his girl-friend, Amanda, and together they too disappeared. That left the four small Keays, who had been in Amanda's care, free to take out their parents. We lunched at the Isle Ornsay Hotel, picked brambles in the hedgerows and raced hairy-marys on the tarmac. Isle Ornsay is part of Skye but it could be almost anywhere in the British Isles. Rabbits played under a spreading sycamore; a man was washing his car while listening to *Any Questions*; the breeze smelt of cow parsley. The whole day was like that, eight hours of limbo in a familiar but now unreal world. It was over before it had begun, leaving just a dim sensation of happy smiles and soft cheeks. When Amanda drove off with the children, leaving us at the shed that was our Broadford base, the memory of school-days was overpowering. It had been our half term, not theirs.

The day had also included a visit to Kylerhea. While the children introduced themselves to Gemini, a sea-lion of television fame who lived in the Nutkins' garage, Terry painted a gloomy picture of Kylerhea politics. He could do nothing about the Dagenham Crofter. The man was Clerk of the Crofting Township – apart from the old lady he *was* the Crofting Township – and he took his office seriously. Given that all the ground you could stand up on was crofting ground, where then were we to have the overnight stance?

'Well you could stick 'em up the back. It's very exposed, mostly rock and there's nothing for 'em to eat. Otherwise your only hope is the flat over there beyond the river. That's Forestry. You could ask in Broadford. Then all you have to do is work out how to get there.'

'Up the back' was hopeless. There was no way you could erect a fence on bare rock and I was sure the boys would force their way into the shelter of Terry's little garden. But 'over there' looked much more inviting, a grassy triangle with the beach, the river and the hill forming its three sides. If the river was up, it would not even be necessary to erect the fence. The Dagenham Crofter's precious acres would be safe and the beasts would get a good bite.

At eight o'clock on Monday morning I was waiting at the door of the Forestry Commission's Broadford office. As usual with the Commission there was no problem; a phone call and permission was graciously given.

'But how are you intending to get there?'

'Down the track – it's marked on the map – and then across the river.'

'Ah, but you see, you'll be needing to clear it with the crofters. You see, it's through the township.'

'But there's only two crofters, and it's a road.'

'Aye but you'll need to speak to them.'

'We have.'

'Well then. You must be knowing the man. We've to be very careful, you see. I can give you the ground. The rest is up to the man.'

By the time I caught up with the drove they were out of Broadford and making good progress along the main road to Kyleakin and the mainland. I thus missed the coffee and drop scones which a Broadford housewife had laid out for the drovers and I missed what had reportedly been a most orderly progress down the main street. There was still a long tail-back of traffic but the motorists were showing no signs of impatience; if anything they were compounding the problem. Unlike the boys, who were sticking to one side of the road and doing exactly as they were asked, cars were nosing about all over the place and blithely ignoring our signals. Anxiety prompted some to park, switch off and wind up the windows, thus blocking half the road and presenting the boys with an irresistible curiosity that had to be minutely inspected. Others drew abreast, wound down the windows and proceeded to photograph and converse. With great difficulty an enormous bus full of Japanese visitors was manoeuvred along the length of the drove only to pull up with a swish of breaks dead in our path. We squeezed slowly past to the whirring of cine cameras. The bus then sounded its horn to overtake again. At that moment a squall strafed the road with hailstones. It was hard to see what was happening but I think it was The Monarch, a quiet beast with a monumental spread of horn, who caught the bus's wing mirror a glancing blow and left the wiggly scratch amidships. It deserved worse.

'There's nothing wrong with ma cow. Ach, she's a great cow. Gavin, now, he just wants her for his dogs, eh John? Come on Matilda. You'll show them.'

George had been leading Matilda along the road on a halter; he was still convinced that she was the natural leader but he felt that she needed instruction in her duties. At the turning for Kylerhea we had stopped for lunch, man and beast huddling in the heather for shelter. Across the road the windsock on the Broadford airstrip was thrashing about like a demented clown.

Between mouthfuls of fruit-cake Gavin exploded with derisive glee. 'Want her for my dogs? You must be joking. There's more meat on a bicycle.'

Since we would not be needing the dogs again that day Gavin volunteered to take the good tidings of the new stance to the Dagenham Crofter. For the rest of the drove the afternoon was as it should be – uneventful. The road, now single track and traffic-free, dawdled gently upwards. A burn on one side and a forestry fence on the other contained the beasts. The sun flicked in and out of the showers and behind us the white-capped waters of Broadford Bay opened into the Sound of Skye, its black and bulky islands – Scalpay, Raasay, Pabay – lying low in the water, a fleet at anchor.

Near the watershed at the head of Glen Arroch JP had erected the big green mess tent single handed – a considerable feat. The ponies were grazing at the roadside and Julia was already brewing soup. It was good to be up in the hills again, good to be just us. A round of self-congratulation seemed in order. Then Gavin reappeared.

'You won't believe this. I mean you just will not believe it.' He was as pink as the sunset and shaking.

'He gave you a dram? He asked for your autograph? We're invited for dinner?'

'Like hell we are. You know what he said? He won't let us through. That's it. He's put a lock on the gate so we can't even get onto that track. Look, I told him – we just wanted to go

down the track (Christ, it's only a few yards) and over the river
to the Forestry. He kept waving this map at me, said the road
belonged to the crofts and that was it. "I'm very sorry," he
kept saying. Who the hell does he think he is? King of
Kylerhea? Oh yes, and then I said we'd use the electric fence
to make sure they didn't stray. "Ah, but that might interfere
with my reception of Radio 3." Yes, I promise you. That's
what he said. "I'd have to complain to the BBC." Honestly.
"I'd have to complain to the BBC." '

George, who said the least, felt the blow the most. He sank
to the ground in a daze, ruffling his grey hair in mystification.
The Dagenham Crofter had committed the two most heinous
crimes in the book. He had come between the beasts and their
grazing and he had tried to frustrate the drove. 'How?' George
kept saying ('how?' means 'why?'). 'How's that? How'ds the
man say that?' That a fellow keeper of livestock, let alone one
of the ever considerate crofters of Skye, could be so bloody-
minded in a matter so vital beggared comprehension.

That night ingenious and excruciating were the retaliatory
gestures which were canvassed into the small hours. We slept
in a fury, woke late, and crawled out to be confronted by a
television camera; I had forgotten that they were coming to
film the frying of the eggs. However, their early start had been
rewarded by something much more newsworthy. Four miles
back up the road they had come across a herd of familiar-
looking Highland cattle grazing placidly beside the Broadford
airstrip. 'Could it be?' they wondered.

It could. Red and yellow wires were festooned along the
roadside; the poles had been dragged with them; there was not
a beast to be seen.

Two hours later as, breakfastless, we drove the boys up hills
that seemed less gentle than yesterday, each of us had his
suspicions. Gavin thought it might have been the BBC. They
were forever looking for action. After the disappointingly
disciplined procession through Broadford who was to say that
they had not decided to contrive something? Julia, who is of a

more trusting nature, blamed the fence. Perhaps it had shorted into the deep wet heather; perhaps those who said that Highlanders would ignore it were right. Both were possible. And were her ponies not still standing obediently beside their picket line, halters securely tied?

For the record, during the whole drove the beasts would break out of the fence only once more. On that occasion they would have ample provocation; in Glen Arroch they had none. They had shelter, water and a bite to eat. It was cold and wet but less so than on most nights. And at midnight they were all comfortably bedded down with the fence still ticking away. I was pretty sure that some time in the night I had heard a car. It was coming up the glen. A charitable explanation would be that it had somehow panicked the beasts.

Curiously, Kylerhea and Glenelg, its opposite number on the mainland, though both scenically delightful, have a long and unenviable reputation for inhospitality. Commanding the Hebridean Bosphorus they seem, like their corridor of churning water, to have regarded the traveller as fair game. At the Ferry Inn, picturesquely perched on a rocky point on the Glenelg side, Johnson and Boswell fared worse than on any other night of their journey. After nearly falling off his horse on the Ratagan pass the Doctor was badly shaken; he felt 'weary and peevish' and had just had a flaming row with his companion. By the time they reached the inn it was dark. The maid showed them to their room – 'damp and dirty with bare walls, a variety of bad smells, a coarse black greasy fir table and forms of the same kind'. From one of the beds leapt an ogre who reminded Boswell of Edgar in *King Lear*; the Doctor thought he was more like Cyclops. 'Of provisions the negative catalogue was very copious. Here was no meat, no milk, no bread, no eggs, no wine. We did not express much satisfaction. Here, however, we were to stay.' Hay, which in September and in such a busy place, should have been plentiful, was also on the negative catalogue. The horses went supperless and the travellers had to send out for the few sheaves necessary for bed-making. On them, Boswell spread out his sheets 'and lay in linen like a gentleman'. Johnson merely wrapped his riding coat round him and burrowed into the hay like a dedicated tramp. Things were that bad.

Fifty years later Dr John MacCulloch, Sir Walter Scott's sleuth and informant in all matters Highland, encountered comparable incivility at the Kylerhea Inn (now the Nutkins' house). On the promise of eggs he waited four hours for breakfast, then got herring. Next day he was presented with a bill for six shillings for his horse's grazing – 'a sum greater than the annual rent of all the grass which he [the proprietor] possessed'. 'In fact poor Roger [the horse] had been turned loose upon the sea-shore to pick up what he could.' MacCulloch paid up but never forgot the injustice nor forgave Mr and Mrs Nicholson their unwarranted spite. Passing through the kyle on a customs launch two years later he told the officers of his misadventure. Without consulting him they promptly put about and headed into the shore. On the reasonable assumption that every Highland hostelry had its stock of illicit whisky they raided the inn. It was a classic 'bust', the Nicholsons howled and MacCulloch enjoyed every minute of it. Had they been Sghianachs the betrayal would have been unforgivable. But then Sghianachs would never have fleeced a traveller. The point about the Nicholsons – and the Dagenham Crofter – was, as MacCulloch put it, that 'they were neither Scot nor Gael'.

5 Downturn Brindle bounds onto the Scottish mainland with encouragement from George

6 The first beasts come ashore from the *Glenmallie* at Glenelg

8

'The art of doing it properly'

KYLERHEA TO KINLOCHOURN

When Dr MacCulloch made his first, unhappy visit to Kylerhea – some time between 1811 and 1821 – the inn there was already 'the Ferry Inn'. There was therefore a ferry and, from what MacCulloch says, it was clearly capable of carrying horses. Any craft that carries horses can also take cattle. The last reference to drovers actually swimming their beasts here dates from 1813 and one can therefore assume that by about 1820, and therefore as the trade approached its climax, droves normally crossed to the mainland by boat. It was from about this date that the longer but less turbulent crossing from Kyleakin to Kyle of Lochalsh, the main ferry route today, began to rival that between Kylerhea and Glenelg, which again suggests that boats had taken over. The silence of that careful observer, Joseph Mitchell, is further evidence that, by the mid-1820s, the transition was complete.

Not that conveying cattle by boat was necessarily easier or safer. The boats used were large, open rowing-boats about forty to fifty feet long and, according to Mitchell, 'of great width of beam'. 'The cattle were fastened with their heads to rings on the gunwale' and to avoid movement were packed as tightly as sardines. Thus twenty might be carried at a time. Alternatively there might be a central partition to which the cattle were tied facing inwards. The floor was deeply strewn with birch saplings or hazel to protect the decking and provide bedding.

Mitchell recalled a near fatal crossing from Jura to the

mainland in a similar boat though fitted with a sail. With a cargo of eighteen beasts, one pony and a bevy of half-drunk drovers the ferryman attempted to sail before a following westerly gale. As the wind began to force the bow under the waves it was discovered that the sail could not be dismantled. Water poured in and, in Mitchell's words, 'there was fear of being swamped'. 'Still the boat flew before the wind; every moment we expected would be our last.' The gale roared, the cattle bellowed as they fought to get free, and Mitchell clung to the pony 'in the hope that if we did go down the creature might swim ashore'. They were saved by one of the drovers who, asserting that authority essential to his profession, simply took command. He proved to be a brilliant helmsman.

> How admirably the drover steered . . . Although some forty years have passed since this incident I shall never forget the Lagg ferry or the gallant Highland drover who by his prompt and decided action was the means under Providence of saving our lives.

An elderly resident of Elgol (on Skye), Mr Lachie MacKinnon, graphically described what could have happened. In the 1920s he was farming on the island of Soay whence his cattle were ferried across to Skye in a rowing boat although by then the practice was to tow it with a launch. MacKinnon was travelling with the cattle in a heavy sea when the boat sprang a leak. It sank so rapidly that there was no chance to release the beasts, all of which drowned. MacKinnon, who, like most islanders, had never learnt to swim, was himself 'like to have followed them'.

> But I kept poppin' up, you see, poppin' up. They [the men in the launch] threw things at me, doors and the like. But I couldn't get to them. You see, they were in fear of hitting me. Yes. And I kept poppin' up. Then they threw a rope.

At Glenelg there is a cobbled ramp which is said to be where the beasts came ashore. It is still in fair condition and was probably used for landing ferried beasts as well as those that swam. Unfortunately the modern concrete slipway has to some extent blocked it off so that it would now be extremely difficult to pilot unroped cattle towards it. More instructive is the corridor of shingle on the Kylerhea side which is thought to have been where the beasts were put into the water. Just south of the modern slipway and below the inn the jagged shoreline of rocks parts to leave a narrow steep-sided passage leading down to and under the water, a sort of roofless corridor with what was presumably easy access from the landward side before the modern road was raised above it. Immediately one can see why, in spite of its dangerous currents, Kylerhea was the preferred place for cattle that were to swim. The passage narrows to the width of two beasts as it enters the water and where the wall on one side is too low it has been built up with chunks of rock. It is thus a perfect funnel, custom-built for launching kine.

Studying it after a steep but disaster-free descent of the Kylerhea glen I began to wonder whether we were not being rather feeble about the swim. The corridor certainly extended into four or five feet of water which would explain how they managed the roping of the beasts so easily; in such ideal handling conditions, the animals being confined but already afloat, they could have been fitted with life-jackets. Accounts differ as to whether the best time for swimming was the high or the low tide. But if, as local opinion insists, it was the low tide, the current which then flows *up* the kyle would not only take the beasts in the desired direction (Kylerhea being not opposite but somewhat below the Glenelg slipway) but would also take them away from the only bit of beach to which they could have turned back. Should they not be roped, any temptation to turn for home would thus be eliminated by the shoreline of forbidding rocks.

Suddenly it all began to make sense. With the tide right and with a few beasts bellowing from the holding area on the other side, it was easy to see how, roped or unroped, 'they'd go'. And what a spectacle. It was the vision of those massively horned heads, tightly bunched and forging imperceptibly through the black water, with the spray leaping at the rocks and the mountains lowering above, which had first opened my eyes to the wonder of Highland droving. Having got this far it seemed absurd to forgo the one and only chance of ever recreating such a scene.

The decision, finally, was made for us. John Grundy, Skye officer of the SPCA, reappeared in his little blue van and announced that the Society must oppose any attempt to swim the kyle. He was probably right and he was extremely sorry. So were we. But I cannot deny that for most of us it was also a relief. Our only concern was to get the beasts to Crieff as safely and authentically as possible. And no drover worthy of the name would have put his cattle in the water once there was a perfectly good ferry in operation.

The last night on Skye we spent camped on a shelf above the Nutkins' house. As darkness fell the kyle twinkled with the lights of trawlers heading north for Kyle of Lochalsh. Immediately below us the empty crofters' cottages dotted the few acres of level ground in as random an arrangement as the stooks of hay in the fields. Silvered by a bright moon and a sharp frost, the scene slipped out of time and context. Although backed by lofty hills this was not some cosy, self-sufficient little glen but a forlorn waiting room. Having climbed Glen Arroch and then dropped steeply down the hillside into Kylerhea there was only one way to go – across the water. It was a place of transit where one waited on a boat or a tide; in the frosty air the whole township seemed locked in a time vacuum, itself waiting on better days, remembering happier times.

Along the road down to the pier our cattle wandered miserably up and down eyeing the rich grazing beyond the Dagenham Crofter's locked gate. After dark we moved them to a derelict sheep fank (or pen), its crumbling drystone walls having been made stockproof with some wooden rails and a few strands of wire. All night, amidst unseasonable flurries of snow, someone kept watch on them; we were taking no chances here. In the morning we left the wire and rails in place. The fank was on land that belonged to the landlord of Kylerhea; it was a way of saying thank you. This, however, did not prevent the Dagenham Crofter from writing to the local press with accusations of our having left the glen strewn with barbed wire.

Curiously he did not mention this when I spoke to him next morning; on the contrary he seemed rather grateful for our co-operation. Perhaps it was because he was so outnumbered. Friends from all over the island had come to say goodbye. There, too, were numerous camp-followers and photographers, the BBC, the SPCA, the police and the coastguard. And just as the last beasts were being loaded a breathless Calum MacDonald, Skye's man of many media, scrambled aboard; Julia's interview for *Woman's Hour* was recorded to a background of scuffles and moos as the ferry chugged across.

There was also an extra drover. Russell Buchanan, the proprietor of a hotel in Argyll and the provider of our ponies and horsebox, had agreed to join us. Besides keeping some cattle of his own he had once worked in a slaughterhouse acquiring there a fearless dexterity in the handling of beasts. He also possessed a genius for improvisation and seemed capable of doing everyone's job as well if not better than they. This was important. In a party of highly individual characters what was needed was 'a steadying influence', a bit of human roughage to stabilise more volatile elements. Russell's inexhaustible supply of ginger wine added a new zest to the whisky just as his passionate commitment to the success of the drove was a timely tonic to the human spirit.

*　　*　　*

Murdo MacKenzie, Master of the *Glenmallie*, normally lays up his boat in September. Before bringing it out to ferry a drove of cattle in October he had had to inform the coastguards who in turn informed NATO command; the kyle is much used by both surface vessels and submarines. But, if I understood him right, the same procedure would have had to have been followed if the beasts had been swum. Might not some unseen radar screen pick up these red hairy shapes and mistake them for torpedoes?

Julia had already been in correspondence with the Ministry of Defence about that scourge of the Highlands, low-flying aircraft. The MoD had promised to try and avoid exercises in our vicinity and, apart from an amazingly silent V bomber in Glen Sligachan, they were as good as their word. Whether the beasts would have been panicked by the scream of a Phantom at zero altitude is thus uncertain but it was surely more probable than a submarine being panicked by a few frantically paddling cattle.

Murdo, however, leaves nothing to chance. Traversing the most demented narrows in Britain in a small and antiquated vessel he can ill afford to take risks. For the cattle he brought sawdust to scatter on the decking and for himself he brought a full packet of cigarettes. He would take just ten beasts at a time and they would be our responsibility although, from the look of them, they would not need to be roped.

On the narrow road we carefully divided the drove into three and shunted the first ten, which included Matilda, von Simpson and all others with a claim to leadership, onto the slipway. They glared at the sea, sniffed at the *Glenmallie*'s ramp where it grated on the rough concrete, and backed away; it looked as if Murdo was going to need his cigarettes. For form's sake we made a second push and obligingly the boys began to climb aboard. Even George could barely disguise his surprise. Patiently they waited while the ponies and a car were smuggled alongside them and then, like happy tourists, they watched the current boiling beneath them and gazed at the receding mountains of Skye.

If cows had elbows they would have been resting them on the railings, such was the contentment of the cargo and the spell of the morning. As the last strands of mist subsided into the water or withdrew into the furthest corries, a dazzling day worthy of the setting slowly asserted itself.

Light more bright than seemed possible in such a deep hollow flooded the scene and leapt from every wave. The snowline, from having been down to sea-level during the night, had slunk back up to the tops leaving a dewy tingle on the rocks and giving an underwater shimmer to the crofting pastures. Such a rich conjunction of restless water, intricate coastline, and menacing mountain, of field and forest, heath and rock, is taxing fare. If only the moment would freeze, the ferry ground, to give one time to digest it. But on the west coast it's like that; always feast or famine. And mostly the latter. To live here is to surrender a large chunk of one's being to the vagaries of a more than vindictive climate. One has to learn to live on two levels, toiling and cursing in a private and tightly wrapped world for three hundred days in the year yet ready to soar without notice to breathless heights of rapture and well-being on any of the remaining sixty-five. No doubt this helps to explain the philosophical and unassertive West Highland temperament. Dispersed to the ends of the earth Highlanders could still retain their identity because they were used to the sensations of constant travel. At home, too, the views had never ceased to surprise and not a day was to be relied on. To survive such wearing uncertainty the native must dig deep into his peaty reserves of individuality and cultivate elaborate shelter belts of routine, religion or preoccupation.

Droving capitalises on such qualities, and the drover's life of dour and dogged patience interspersed with outbursts of activity and conviviality was an exact replica of the uncertain West Highland climate. Weather and scenery, calling and character, all seemed to work into the same pattern. The intricate complementalities were overwhelming. It is, though, possible to feel trapped by such a comprehensive environment. Like the rice farmer knee-deep in warm alluvial mud amidst post-monsoon vapours, one could find so neatly balanced an ecosystem claustrophobic. It was, I suppose, the ultimate contradiction; on the one hand we desperately

wanted to be part of the place, to imbibe 'the ancient art and
science of droving', to adapt to the cattle and the countryside
and to share in their rhythms and patterns; but on the other
hand, none of us wanted to surrender to them completely. We
could no more become philosophical about the weather than
make a livelihood out of droving. And we didn't want to.

Camped that night on the shore at Glen Bernera a mile from
the Glenelg slipway, I watched a red and white supply vessel
impertinently trying to force its way through the kyle against
the current. Measured by a row of equally spaced cormorants
on an intervening ledge it moved just a single draped wingspan
in the first hour. Without the cormorants one would have
thought it stationary. But by the end of the second hour, with
the current presumably changing, it had shot past eight whole
birds and was disappearing round the headland. Evidently
intruders, however garish, however impertinent or ambiva-
lent, had to come to terms with the environment.

Over the next three days, liking it for the most part but
occasionally loathing it, we did learn something of droving.
Side-stepping and climbing against the grain of the country
the drove wound through Glenelg to Glen Beag, then climbed
round Ben Sgritheall to Arnisdale and climbed again over to
Kinlochourn. Each day was a long and mildly tiring slog
interrupted by moments of excitement, pleasantry, despair
and rapture. In Glenelg the sun lit on a row of chestnut trees
and made their leaves shine like horse brasses. The locals leant
on their gates and we trooped in for potato scones and Nescafé
while the boys went paddling on the shore. At Arnisdale it was
after-dinner mints and a glass of port at the big house with JP
convulsed over having shaken hands with a girl called 'Froxie'
and Julia trying to sip from a miniscule coffee cup without
parading her grimy fingernails. I remember George detaining
a bus and three cars while he stood in the middle of the road
and held me by the elbow lest the thread of his story be
broken. I remember hearing the familiar squeak of leather and
basketwork and looking round to find that the ponies had

donned wellingtons – or rather thick peaty coatings that reached to their hocks.

There were moments of intense frustration – as when the first two hours of daylight were wasted looking for the beasts before we realised that their gate had been left open all night; by then they were three miles away in the wrong direction. (There was never any problem finding them; you simply followed the cowpats.) Or there was the time when, reluctant to surrender height unnecessarily, we contoured round above the ponies and found ourselves stranded on a ledge with no alternative but to retrace a thousand painful steps. The passes were so steep it was hard to credit reports that they had been regularly used by drovers. And there were descents so rocky that I had nightmares about broken legs, humane killers, and steaks for breakfast.

But mostly there was just the uneventful and steady plod – a pace of perhaps one and a half miles an hour broken by halts every half hour or so. With a hundred and fifty miles still to go it was a difficult pace to keep to. Impatience could sometimes be vented by scouring to left and right to hound the laggards. One, a stocky red bullock with an ungainly roll to his gait, was intent on grazing every step of the way. This preoccupation with feeding won him the nickname of Gavin; left to his own devices, he would have cut as trim a swathe as a lawnmower right across the Highlands. Often there was no need for such zealous activity on our part. Time would reveal that the drove moved in three basic conformations of which the first, the column, required no sideways excursions at all.

Recalling his droving youth for the benefit of posterity and the School of Scottish Studies the late Dugald MacDougall of Argyll gave the best description of droving that exists. He was ninety when, in 1956, he confided it to a tape-recorder, the first he had ever seen.

> One would think that there was nothing but drive and force them on with a stick, but that wasn't allowed at all. They'd go quite nicely when they were left alone. The man that was in front – they

didn't all stay behind – he took maybe twelve or so of the first cattle on, and the rest followed; and if these went into a gap, or found an open gate, and went in, you had only to get twelve out, whereas if you were all behind, you would have to get the whole fifty or sixty and spend time to get them back out again. There was an art in doing it right, properly; even suppose one would think it a simple thing, there was an art in doing it properly too, to give man and beast a chance, yes.

Moving cattle from Argyll to Falkirk in the 1890s meant following well-defined drove roads and carriageways. As we had discovered on Skye, on any kind of road the cattle tended to string out in one or two columns – with Matilda sometimes making a third. If the road was tarmac or gravel they filed along the grass verge; if it was a soft footpath they marched along the middle. The smaller beasts would be at the back with the laggards – the tiny twins Ickle Brindle and Ickle Red, with the red bullock Gavin and a bony yellow beast with a mean kick. In the middle walked the quieter boys including the top-heavy Monarch. And upfront were the strongest and most assertive, von Simpson, Goldie, Upturn Brindle and Downturn Brindle.

As MacDougall emphasised, the secret of this formation was to have one man behind the leading beasts. He usually cut in after the first eight or ten and, if the idea was to push along, he kept these beasts moving, allowing the odd one to slip behind rather than lose momentum. When there were only two or three left in front, and they no doubt hesitating, he retreated down the line and cut in again behind the ten leaders. With someone well in front to scout the ground and someone at the back to see that all were moving easily, there was no need for dogs. A good pace could be set and maintained; but it allowed for no wayside grazing and could be tiring for the beasts. Halts were therefore essential.

The same principle of cutting out the leading beasts and working them across first was also used for obstacles of any sort – burns, steep bits, bridges, peat hags, cattle grids. It succeeded because the boys were now acquiring that spontaneous cohesion without which droving would be impossible. In our ignorance we had been looking for one undisputed leader and waiting for a pecking order to emerge. But evidently herd politics rested on consensus; the willingness of all to stick together was much more important than whatever authority a leader might impose. We had done the beasts a grave injustice. The subtlety of their relationships and their intricate system of checks and balances allowed for the dignity of each individual member. None was invariably put upon and the smallest would sometimes take the fore. Even Matilda was never treated as an outcaste; gradually if reluctantly she would assume her place in society.

The second, and more natural, droving formation illustrated this egalitarianism well. In open country where there was no confining track, across moorland or on a straight climb at the head of a glen, the beasts usually fanned out in a wide and shallow arc, or bow. References to 'a bow of cattle' and to drovers as 'bowmen' may well derive from this habit. Essentially it was a grazing formation, each beast having his own foraging area whilst remaining in touch with the rest of the herd. Where the ground permitted, it was probably the ideal type of progression. The beasts moved at a snail's pace, they got plenty to eat, and the drovers, working to and fro behind them, got plenty of exercise. With the addition of the prompting needed to keep them on course, it was the sort of pattern they would naturally have adopted on any new pasture. No beast, or beasts, orchestrated it and each could assert his integrity within the herd.

It was, however, somewhat unmanageable. On broken ground the extremities of the bow might get left behind and in deep heather the drovers would soon be collapsing with exhaustion. Climbing the 1500-foot Bealach Aoidhdailean pass, for example, we found that at whatever point in the bow you pushed, the beasts fell away sideways. It was like breakers swooping up to the tideline and then slithering away at a tangent. After an hour of this, with frayed tempers but practically no progress to show for it, Gavin rightly insisted that it was a case for the dogs. We were imperiously ordered out of the way as Jody swept down for the gather.

With a dog on their heels the cattle adopted the third formation, the pack. On ground as steep as the pass they had to be unashamedly pushed. Gavin, staying well in front, shouted, whistled and swore as dog or dogs flew right and left keeping the pack tight and scrum-like. But on gentler ground such aggressive handling was unnecessary. Jody could be left to work the beasts at her own pace. The pack was then much looser; she seldom needed to snap at a beast's heels and there was less danger of getting a kick in return. It was still a faster pace than was possible in column or bow formation and it was of course much less labour-intensive. One man and a good dog could handle fifty beasts and cover up to twenty miles a day.

According to one of the newspapers, on the day we crossed from Skye 'a real farmer-drover' reached Kinlochourn after driving his beasts across the roadless Knoydart peninsula for two days with the help of a single collie. Those who ridiculed the ballyhoo of our 'Famous Highland Drove' invariably quoted some such example and many of the old boys who gave us the benefit of their experience were recalling similar feats. After the railways had reached the west coast in the late nineteenth century droving became simply a matter of getting your beasts to the nearest station. It might take two days and the idea was to get it over as quickly as possible. Hence they used dogs and aimed at at least fifteen miles a day. Feeding, lameness and stress were not overwhelming considerations since beasts in good condition should suffer little in a mere forty-eight hours. Besides, the rail journey was likely to be infinitely more harmful in this respect. But such methods and such attitudes would have proved disastrous on the long hike to Falkirk or Crieff. 'The great secret', according to Dugald MacDougall and, indeed, to every other witness of the long distance droves 'was to take them there [Falkirk] as good looking as they were when they left home . . . They were

[then] in full bloom, and full of flesh and hair. If you sweated them, the hair dropped down and never got up again into the same.'

For any distance of more than three days or fifty miles the health and condition of the cattle became the paramount factor. As we were learning from experience, there were times when we had to push the cattle and times when without dogs we would have had to abandon the planned route. But as experience would also show, to have used dogs any more than we did would have been catastrophic. Gavin, the dog-handler and the hard man in such matters, and George, the old time stockman and self-appointed spokesman for the beasts, were both right in their different ways. It could sometimes be a problem to decide between them – a problem in which the advice of Chris, the vet, and the handling experience of Russell proved crucial. But the problem was as nothing compared to the fortuitous triumph of having secured the help of two men whose very different ideas on the subject offered the chance of a happy and, I believe, authentic medium.

*   *   *

'Is this no the glen we was coming down yesterday? And back there's where we turned down from the pass. Must be. Tell me, John, am I right now?'

'Afraid so, George.'

'Well,' he took off his cap and flicked it back on again, 'well, how did we do that? I mean, how didna we just keep straight on? We'd no need to go down all them rocks to Arnisdale. We could have stopped the night up here. Aye, fine we could.'

'But what about the tents? And where would we have put the beasts?'

'Och, one night wouldna have hurt us. Someone could have kept an eye on the beasts. Much better than all that rock.'

When I had walked the ground the year before I had been obsessed with bogs. The top of the glen had looked exceptionally boggy while the track that bypassed it by falling a thousand feet to Arnisdale and then climbed a thousand feet back up again was good firm rock. As for sleeping without tents, the inevitable consequence of being out of reach of the Land Rover, that all depended on the weather. Last night had been dry. It would not have been had we been committed to sleeping out. The possibility of getting benighted was always there; indeed it was a good deal closer than either of us realised. But it was not something to be invited. Quite apart from the personal discomfort it would also mean the ponies having to make a double run with hay and cattle cobs or the beasts going hungry. 'There was an art in doing it properly too, to give man and beast a chance, yes.'

It was Day Twelve and we had now covered about sixty of the two hundred miles to Crieff. We were following a scarcely visible path which meandered across the floor of the glen, now more a high and open basin than a valley. Ahead the lip of the basin concealed the chasm which is Loch Hourn; everyone had been warned that the day would end with the most perilous descent of the whole journey. But up here, with the sun low to the right and the going as ideal as could be, there was no temptation to dwell on uncertainties. From the hills on either side stags bellowed their claim to the shy hinds on the heights above. Sharp as a bark, wild as a roar, their calls reverberated in the still air. It was as if the mountains themselves were giving voice in savage rage. It broke from the interstices of the rock like seismic thunder and earthed in the region of one's shoulder-blades long before ear or brain could explain it. Even then there was a need to scan the mountain until the culprit was satisfactorily identified. No sound, except perhaps the anguished sigh of the seal, is more redolent with the unnerving quality of the primeval.

Curiously it bothered the cattle not at all. The horn of a car or the bark of a dog would get their instant attention; a moo would send them into paroxysms of excitement. But the roaring which had their drovers in such a high state of tension appeared to pass them by. By contrast with the rocky and reverberating heights the scene below was one of unreal tranquillity. The low and liquid sun worked its alchemy bathing man and beast in gold. We were a stream of gold moving across a cloth of gold. Deer grass – which is more like hair than grass – and the unassuming bog asphodel carpeted the ground with their dying splendour. Even the peaty burns flowed the amber of whisky while, beside them, gnarled birches dripped with autumnal yellow. Beyond the swaying file of beasts I could just make out the ponies, Mhari by the side-slung panniers which made her look like a drum-major's mount, and Rona by the slate grey of her coat. Eilidh, the bay, was just another spurt of gold. They climbed out of the hollow, then paused on the lip, heads down. Then they plunged out of sight.

Half an hour later we too crested the ridge, re-formed, and set about the descent. According to the map, now metric, the track here drops 250 metres vertically in a horizontal distance of 700 metres. That does not even make a one in two slope; to the eye it looked more than one in one. The conformation is that of a long straight gully up which there was once a beautifully constructed path which looped from side to side with an even and comparatively gentle gradient. Where its neat stone banking and cutting is still visible it is about four feet wide, the ideal width for beasts or even laden ponies in single file. No doubt both size and alignment were dictated by the needs of drovers. More recently the North of Scotland Hydro-Electric Board have brought their pylons up the self-same gully and, to maintain them, have been wont to drive their tracked vehicles straight up. The resultant 'track', aided by the formidable rainfall, is now a long treacherous rock slide scoured deep into the ground and bisecting the loops of the old drove path in about twenty places.

On the old path we were safe enough provided the beasts kept moving and therefore did not bunch. But at every intersection with the rock slide they had to be coaxed down onto the treacherous mixture of scree and boulders and then back up at the right point to strike the old path again. Even with four men to thirty beasts it was a desperate struggle. Matilda, a look of wild panic in her eyes, baulked at every crossing. Together with some of the younger boys she held back as long as she could and kept Chris or George a hundred feet above the rest of us with the very real danger of dislodging rocks in our direction.

When a large red beast ventured out of line and tottered onto a little promontory of uneroded aggregate I knew he had had it. There was no way he could turn and on either side an eight-foot drop fell sheer onto the rock slide. We stood beneath, powerless to help but willing to chance shoulders, hips, anything, to break his fall. At last he made his move, front legs crumbling the edge with all his weight on them and digging into the resultant landslide till he was performing a handstand. At this point he slewed his weight into the hill, wrenched front legs out, and landed in a cataract of stone facing downhill. He got up, embarrassed at what had been a hideously ungraceful manoeuvre, but miraculously unharmed. In the excitement I had forgotten all about St Bridget.

When at last we reached the wooded policies above Kin-lochourn the sun had gone and the waters of the loch were already grey with twilight. From Julia came word that the big house was deserted; to avoid dropping even further down to the lochside and then having to climb out again in the morning we should continue along the hydro track which now contoured round the glen. We would all meet up where it presumably joined the tarmac road beside a small lochan. This was an old stance; there was a fenced park for the beasts and there was a derelict bothy if we needed shelter; it was called Coireshubh on the map.

Had any of us ever walked the hydro track we would have realised that it was death to cattle. With scant regard for the landscape it had been cut, blasted and gouged straight out of the hillside. To maintain its level it faithfully followed the

7 Von Simpson (centre), a beast of outstanding character who was much fancied as
the leader of the drove

8 Climbing from Balvraid near the head of Glen Beag in Wester Ross

contours even to doubling round precipices and cutting far back into each fold in the mountain. The surface was the blasted rock – jagged lumps and slabs still loose, without a vestige of soil or turf and more cruel on the feet than railway clinkers. As a feat of defiant engineering it deserved a place on the map. Perhaps it was too new to be included, or perhaps it was simply too unspeakable.

After an hour's dismal progress it was too dark to see how much further it went or how far we had come. I rushed on ahead to get torches but it was half an hour before I finally blundered onto the tarmac. And it was now pitch dark.

'Anyone there?' I thought I had heard the snort of a pony. It still felt idiotic to be shouting a neighbourly greeting into such a black and hostile emptiness.

'Yes, it's me.' Julia's whispered and ever so calm reply came from about two feet away.

'Where the hell is everyone? And where's the bothy? It's going to take hours to get the boys round here. Christ Almighty what a track. We need torches, whisky . . .'

'Calm down, calm down. JP's had an accident. The trailer's stuck half way down the hill and the bothy's over there.'

'What? Where? Bloody Hell.'

Headlights were approaching – an amazing stroke of luck so near the end of this desolate cul-de-sac. I begged a lift down to the scene of the accident. The horsebox had two punctures, a twisted mudguard and a bent axle. On a road so steep and narrow that it was scarcely safe for cars, it had clipped the stones on the outer edge. Thankfully the Land Rover was all right. Russell ran me back up and, with bottle and torch, I set off back to the beasts. It was now eight o'clock; we had been on the move for thirteen hours.

With the torch I could get a better idea of the horrors of the track. There were two raging torrents to be crossed and except for the last few yards it was rock all the way. At night, with exhausted beasts and exhausted drovers it was just not possible. The beasts were lying down so often that Chris, Gavin and

George had managed barely quarter of a mile in the past hour. For the first and only time we decided to chance it and leave them be. It was an admission of defeat. Half-way back to the road Russell met us with the Land Rover. He had already salvaged the trailer and was now intent on salvaging the beasts, the idea being to drive behind them and light their way with the headlights. Had the cattle been up to walking and had the track been motorable this would have been a stroke of genius. But we were beyond road-building. Already Russell was having to leap out every few yards with a crowbar – and he had not yet reached the first of the torrents. Reluctantly he somehow got the thing turned and we headed for the bothy.

Julia and JP had also risen to the crisis. A fire was going, the food was on, six inches of sheep shit were being heroically scraped from the floor, and bales of hay wedged into the sashless windows. We chased whisky macs with cups of tea and felt better. It was crazy to worry about the beasts. They were too tired to feed, never mind stray. And if they did, they could only go forwards or backwards along the track, a far from inviting prospect.

Rice and goulash followed; there was the usual bickering about who snored loudest and where the culprits should lay their sleeping bags. Outside it was dry and quiet.

'What do you think then, John?'

'I think I'll go back. Just to be sure, you know.'

'Aye, well you bring the cratur and I'll get ma kettle.'

Not even George believed it was necessary. But you couldn't be sure. Something might startle the beasts and it was a bad place to be startled. It was also Kinlochourn whence seventeen of them had originally come. The field in which they had been gathered for our first inspection was just down the road; at the time I had hardly dared open the gate their horns looked so ferocious. If at first light tomorrow they got a whiff of familiar pastures heaven knew where they would get to. It was not a heroic gesture. Sleep was going to be impossible knowing they were out there unattended.

9

'Keep their feet right and all will go well'

KINLOCHOURN TO GREENFIELD

To have taken a drove of cattle across the Highlands without spending at least one night out on the hill would have been a serious omission. From Dugald MacDougall's account of droving in the 1890s it seems clear that all the stances in Argyll were then enclosed. ('There's a place – I can see it yet – where we went . . . The stance came down to the road but halfway up the hill it was fenced off. They couldn't get out of it altogether but they had plenty of room, yes, they had plenty of room.') In such a place there was no need for drovers to sleep beside their cattle. But this was probably not the case a century earlier or a hundred miles to the north. Here too drovers would have made every effort to reach the recognised halting places which were usually natural holding areas with water, grazing and shelter to settle the beasts and with perhaps a cliff or a river to help contain them. But even given the greater number of cottages and shielings in those days drovers usually slept out – to protect the cattle as well as to prevent their straying.

Wrapped in his plaid on a bed of springy heather the Highlander seems to have been as comfortable as his beasts. If the wind was particularly keen he first dipped his plaid in the burn; the wet thickened the tweed and made it more windproof. Better still, if the night was cold enough, the dampened plaid froze round him providing a stiff insulating cocoon not unlike our Maxproof outfits. Lieutenant Burt, the English officer who in the early eighteenth century found the mountains so repulsive, took a great delight in cataloguing the hardiness of the people. When, having wound their sodden plaids round them, a party of Highlanders lay down to sleep, 'their bodies made a steam like that of a boiling kettle'. If there was snow on the ground you could always tell where travellers had slept by their thaw marks.

Burt also gives a version of a story so popular that however suspect its origin it must have come uncomfortably close to reality. During a winter foray against one of his neighbours a MacDonald chieftain ordered his men to roll him a snowball by way of a pillow. The men were aghast; were their ears deceiving them? 'Now we must despair,' they murmured. 'Who can think of victory when our chief is become so effeminate he needs a pillow to sleep on.' Later versions ascribe the story to the Camerons of Lochiel with a son of Lochiel rolling himself the pillow and his father kicking it from under his head with a curt rebuke – 'You grow effeminate, sir'.

The night of October 17th was mild, overcast, and mercifully dry until just before dawn. We found the cattle still scattered along the track exactly as we had left them; they had simply flopped down on the hardcore. Above the track the ground rose precipitously with a tangle of half-fallen trees leaning out of the hill; below it a grassy slope appeared to slither away down to the floor of the glen. Down there, in the hollow at the head of Loch Hourn, there were green meadows and there were other cattle – usually an irresistible combination. Tonight the boys were past caring.

The breeze toyed with our fire and then died away into the hills. A solitary light in the glen below went out. We talked and drank and dozed, with frequent excursions to collect more firewood and to check the beasts. Only the stags kept the vigil with us, roaring back and forth across the void. Like other west coast sea lochs, Loch Hourn once supported a thriving community. Up its long arm of water came vast shoals of herring which became so tightly packed in the upper reaches that 'the boats could not force their way through'. In 1772

Thomas Pennant watched over a hundred boats at work. On the shore at Kinlochourn the fires burnt through the night and at dawn all hands turned to the gutting and salting of the catch. The contrast between the extreme wildness of the setting, with the mountains pressing close on all sides, and this unexpected scene of industry made a great impression on him. But in reflecting that 'there is no part of our dominions so remote, so inhospitable and so unprofitable as to deny employ and livelihood to thousands' he tempted fate too far.

Pennant also dutifully enquired after the Loch Hourn *glaslich*, 'a dreadful spectre which haunts these hills in the form of a great dog, or of a man, or of a thin gigantic hag'. Then as now, 'though the night was most excessive dark', the creature failed to appear. For my part I was less worried about the *glas-lich* than about our brownie. Only Loch Hourn has the *glas-lich* but every Highland croft and household should have its brownie. Kindly and ever willing he takes on the drudgery of daily life, washing up, tidying around, mucking out. He is inconspicuous, efficient and asks only that you take him not for granted. In short he is so like JP that the following description from C. E. G. Cumming's *In The Hebrides* may do duty for both.

> In every case the description of this creature is the same; he is like a dwarfish human being, covered with long hair and breathing heavily; having, moreover, large eyes and great strength which he willingly employs for any mortal to whom he takes a fancy, working for him hard and faithfully year after year; but nevertheless apt to be sullen and morose and, on slight provocation, to depart forever.

In a droving context the brownie's role was particularly unenviable. Besides endlessly unloading and loading a ton of equipment, pitching and striking tents, and trundling Land Rover and horsebox up and down appalling tracks, JP was in charge of feeding logistics. At various farms and depots across the Highlands sacks of specially formulated cattle cobs plus pony nuts and dog meal had been dumped by our agricultural sugar daddies, Scottish Agricultural Industries. Additionally we were uplifting hay at numerous points. With the beasts getting through three bales and two sacks a day and with the available capacity of the trailer limited to about ten of each, this side of the operation demanded careful planning and a lot of driving. JP had been doing it for two weeks and he had had enough. The accident tonight had been the final straw. Brownies work on the principle that the jobs they do best are the jobs that go unnoticed. Hence his acute embarrassment when all attention – plus some disparagement – was suddenly focused on the ruptured trailer.

'Sullen and morose' is probably an exaggeration but our brownie was, also, noticeably piqued. As a driver rather than a drover, and having a French name rather than a Scottish one, he had long since resigned himself to being passed over by newsmen and well-wishers. If anything he relished his role as the outsider. He asked only that the rest of us respect his stand and patiently suffer his occasional and well-aimed jibes. In short, he was our electric fence; twelve volts of withering sarcasm was a small price to pay for having one's sense of proportion restored. But increasingly the twelve volts were proving insufficient. Hardened skins and shortened tempers no longer responded so obligingly. Our brownie was not being appreciated and appeared ready indeed 'on slight provocation, to depart forever'.

The only solution was to reallocate responsibilities. George was to leave us in the morning for a sabbatical week and Chris's girl-friend, another vet from Orkney, would be taking his place. With Russell equally capable as drover, driver or ponyman we had a much more flexible team. The sensible thing then was to abandon restrictive practices and enable everyone, including JP, to shuffle responsibilities. Henceforth, with the exception of Gavin who was restricted by his dogs, we would all do turn about.

I looked at my watch; it was five o'clock, the drizzle was turning to rain and, though far from light, it was definitely less dark. The beasts were beginning to stir. The whisky was finished. We unpacked the fire, rounded up the boys and headed them towards breakfast. In the grey and patient dawn the track was as hideous as ever. One of the bullocks, an almost chestnut beast, was noticeably limping and several others looked as if they were feeling their feet. We took it as gently as we could.

Half-way back Julia met us. She had sacrificed at least an hour's sleep to stumble out into the dark and the wet to look for us. Her hair was hanging in long limp rat's-tails and a drop of rain was wobbling on the end of her nose. I wanted very much to hug her.

★   ★   ★

Almost every glen in the West Highlands is reputedly the wettest in Britain; Glen Etive, Glen Coe, Glen Nevis and Glen Sligachan all have this doubtful claim to celebrity. But, for the record, the cup – or rather the bucket – rightfully belongs to Glen Quoich, four miles east of the Coireshubh bothy. Professor Fraser Darling gives its annual rainfall as 'up to 225 inches'. (Edinburgh and London have averages of about 30 inches.) Mountains are notorious for their microclimates and this figure is no doubt a very localised reading. Glen Quoich is at the head of Glen Garry; at the mouth of the glen some twenty miles to the east the average figure is probably no more than 50 inches.

Nevertheless 225 inches, nearly 19 feet, is a daunting statistic. It puts Glen Quoich in the same league as parts of equatorial West Africa or Assam's Cherrapunji, supposedly the world's leader with an average of 426 inches. Unlike these places, in Glen Quoich it rains often as well as hard; there is no such thing as a dry month. Dr MacCulloch once asked a girl who was weeding potatoes beside Loch Hourn how long the snow lay on these hills in winter. ' "Weel I wot," was the answer, "it never gangs till the rain comes." ' But the Argyllshire version of this anecdote would have been more appropriate

– Visitor: 'Does it always rain like this in Inverary (or Dalmally, Oban, Glen Coe etc.)?' Local: 'Och no no, not by any means. You see, sometimes it snows.'

In Glen Quoich and through most of Glen Garry it rained on October 18th and 19th continuously and with monsoon intent. After feeding and resting the beasts at Coireshubh, Gavin and Chris set off to walk them round the long and dreary north shore of Loch Quoich and then along the almost level upper reaches of Glen Garry. They would be following the single-track road but in some places there was soft going on the unfenced grass alongside. The only hazard was likely to be other cattle; it could be a busy day for the dogs. Julia agreed to bring on the ponies while Russell and I coaxed the trailer to a Spean Bridge garage. We had also to collect hay and make final arrangements for the two stances needed in Glen Garry.

According to Lachlan Fletcher, one of Arnisdale's few remaining residents, we should not have been going down Glen Garry at all. Fifty years ago he had walked beasts from his native village to the market in Fort William. He remembered it well and insisted that the old drove route between Kinlochourn and Spean Bridge went much further south from this point by way of the west end of Loch Quoich, Glen Kingie and Loch Arkaig. Studying the map this looked like an unnecessary detour if not an impossibility since the western end of Loch Quoich fingers deep into the sheer and trackless mountains of Knoydart. Why didn't he follow the road? It was more direct, more level and had originally been laid out by Thomas Telford at the beginning of the nineteenth century.

Telford and his disciples, John and Joseph Mitchell, had been much concerned with channelling the droving traffic. Although the main purpose of their roads, bridges and canals (including the Caledonian Canal) was to provide employment and so discourage emigration, much was made of the benefits likely to accrue to the only existing trade of any importance, the export of cattle and sheep. Besides opening communication with the remotest districts, Telford saw his job as:

To explore and establish general lines of practicable communication which as Drove Roads might best accommodate those extensive tracts from whence the Black Cattle and Sheep are sent to the markets in the southern parts of Scotland.

From the Kylerhea–Glenelg crossing the cattle of Skye and the Outer Hebrides were already passing over to Kinlochourn and then on by a variety of routes to cross the Great Glen at Spean Bridge. The Glen Garry road was designed to direct this flow down past Tomdoun whence a further road was to cut the corner above Invergarry and take the traffic over to Achnacarry and Spean Bridge.

Relying heavily on the reports of Telford and his assistants, Professor Haldane constructed his scheme of Highland drove routes. Without his book it would have been impossible to trace out an authentic route and without Haldane's scholarship Scottish droving would still be a matter for conjecture. But the book did pose certain problems and these problems were about to give us real concern.

Initially, I had planned our route on the assumption that droves followed drove roads and that drove roads were well-marked tracks which were gradually improved by the likes of Thomas Telford. In the Lowlands and in England drove roads are still often recognisable because bounded by hedges, fences or embankments. But having walked a few of the pre-Telford Highland drove 'roads' I realised it was more appropriate to talk of drove 'routes'. Except where the road-builders had adopted the same line they were not obvious. Often they consisted of no more than a few rocks laid across soft ground, fording-places on the burns, and a bit of road-building where the natural gradient, as at Kinlochourn, was too steep for safety. In between there might be miles of open country with no clearly defined track at all, and evidence to suggest that each drove took a different route. This made sense. If the object was to exploit the wayside grazing why follow in the muddy footprints of the drove in front?

But I was still influenced by the notion that droves ought to

follow drove 'roads'. I was also obsessed by the dangers of soft
ground. I had even planned the original route to take in a few
tracks of modern construction – forestry and hydro roads –
rather than chance our luck on open ground.

Now, after a taste of the Skye roads and of the hydro track
at Kinlochourn, I was having second thoughts. Roads,
whether made or unmade, ancient or modern, were not to the
beasts' liking and therefore, presumably, never were. There
was a case for treating the reports of Telford and Mitchell with
some caution. Where their new roads provided bridges and
ample roadside grazing they were no doubt welcomed. But
where they offered a hard gravel surface instead of grass or
heather they were not. According to one nineteenth-century
observer:

> He [the drover] prefers, when a choice offers, the grassy pathways
> which are more agreeable to the hoofs of the animals entrusted to
> his care and at the same time afford them a mouthful of food.
> Hence he usually chooses the by-roads as the hard and dusty
> highways are injurious to the hoofs of the cattle and afford little
> nourishment.

And where these new roads encouraged landowners to pro-
hibit free passage by the multiplicity of traditional routes and
to restrict or charge for the roadside grazing they were a
menace. The provision of better roads, far from facilitating the
droving trade, could be seen as part of the movement to
confine it and so free the land for other uses, especially sport.
If this was the case it also followed that it was in the interests
of both road-builders and landowners to oversimplify the existing network of drove routes when projecting the benefits of
a new road. While Telford, and hence Haldane, implied that
from Kinlochourn the usual route was down Glen Garry, it
was still possible that the old drover from Arnisdale was right.

He was certainly right about the topography. The route
round the west end of Loch Quoich to Glen Kingie might look
impossible on a modern map but was, in fact, eminently
feasible fifty years ago. Loch Quoich, like many other High-

land lochs, is no longer as nature intended. Its vast and many-fingered expanse of water is the result of a Hydro-Electric dam which has raised the level by some forty metres.

At one point on its desolate north shore the road suddenly passes from treeless scarps of rock and heather to clumps of windswept rhododendron. These unnatural shrubs are all that remain above water of the gracious policies of Glen Quoich Lodge, the home of Edward Ellice MP whose house parties were once the most fashionable in the West Highlands. When Joseph Mitchell stayed here in 1850 he found himself the only guest without a title. Between 'intellectual communings' there was 'boating on the lake for the ladies' and 'healthful sport' for the gentlemen. Today a less probable spot for dazzle and dalliance is unimaginable. Exposed, featureless and lifeless it looks like a prime landing site for creatures from another planet. The forty extra metres of water which submerged the house and turned this paradise into a moonscape also obliterated the old drove routes along with the lochside meadows and the crofting townships. The surface area of the loch doubled; a two-mile arm of water severed the track to Glen Kingie. Before the flood, five hundred people once emigrated from Glen Quoich in a single year and still the place was well populated. Today the population is nil.

Considering the outcry against the Forestry Commission's insensitive treatment of the countryside it seems odd that the North of Scotland Hydro-Electric Board has never been compelled to make ecological amends for its depredations. In many ways submerging the floor of these glens in water is worse than submerging their sides in sitka spruce. Flora, fauna, pasture and amenity are always richest where there is shelter and depth of soil. But flood a glen, like Quoich, to a level at which the concave slopes of the glen give way to rock and scree and there is no hope of waterside vegetation spontaneously relocating itself. The situation is made worse by the fact that these artificial lochs have no permanent shoreline. Depending on rainfall the water level may vary from week to week by as much as twenty feet. Thus the loch is rimmed with a sometimes wide scar of rock and boulder as uncongenial to the eye as it is to every form of waterside life. A similar fate has befallen the nearby lochs of Cluanie and Loyne. Loch Garry, on the other hand, has a constant shoreline and has been little tampered with. The contrast could hardly be more dramatic. In spite of vast tracts of forestry Glen Garry is spectacularly beautiful while Glen Quoich is a desert in all but rainfall.

Whether drovers had always preferred Lachlan Fletcher's Glen Kingie route to that down Glen Garry is unclear. It could be that they adopted it only after Telford had built his Glen Garry road. But at least we now knew that in following a route that was both authentic and practicable the conformation of lochs could not be taken for granted. Even in Perthshire Loch Lyon and then Loch Lednock would pose serious problems. In both cases the old drove route lay under the water and the alternative tracks were dangerous and unsuitable for cattle.

★   ★   ★

On October 20th the drove moved slowly on down Telford's road. Now a single track of tarmacadam, its twenty unfenced miles running the length of Glen Garry make it one of the most striking roads in Scotland. It is also one of the quietest, ending, as it does, in that spectacular descent into the cul-de-sac that is Kinlochourn. We met the postman heading west and an hour or so later he overtook us heading east; there was no other traffic. Down from the high ground on the left burns dashed in frothy boisterous spate to form up in the dead ground at the foot of the hill. Thence they advanced more self-consciously to glide along the avenues of sombre alder which bisected the roadside pastures. As they slid, now deep and disciplined, beneath sturdy stone bridges, our beasts peered over the parapets to marvel at such a fine example of responsibly behaved water. A hundred yards more, past silver birches royal with autumn colour, they dutifully surrendered to the authority of the Garry river.

Unlike most west coast rivers the Garry flows east. Around Coireshubh some of the burns which feed into Loch Quoich and thence into the Garry begin only three or four miles from the sea in Loch Hourn. Yet because of the lie of the ground their waters must travel some sixty miles round by lochs Garry, Oich and Lochy before they finally reach the sea in Loch Linnhe. This phenomenon may help to explain the rather un-west coast feel of Glen Garry. The river, instead of being direct and impetuous, is broad and placid. In places, as it meanders between marshy banks, it could be a wide chalk stream. Round elegant islets, some crowned with Scots pines, it swirls in silky swoops. No crashing cataracts here, no vulgar rocks scarring its calm. Even the point at which it enters Loch Garry is indeterminate. Below Tomdoun the river widens for the umpteenth time and simply forgets to contract again. Woodland, pasture and forestry continue to alternate pleasingly along its banks and on either side the hills march along at the same respectful distance.

Such a surfeit of grand scenery, enhanced by having as companions creatures who epitomised its quiet glory, induced a mindless torpor. I wrenched myself from both the scene and the mood and sped ahead to arrange planking for a cattle-grid. The grid was on the bailey bridge which spans the loch's waist between two picturesque promontories. It was the only grid on the whole route which could not be bypassed by an adjacent gate and fortunately we had noticed it well in advance. I tried out the planks, kindly supplied by a local farmer, and wondered how the beasts would take to the bridge. (Bridges as such they did not mind; but they disliked loose decking and preferred not to be able to see through it.) Then I walked back up the road towards Tomdoun.

After yesterday's deluge the temperature was down but the air was clear and the sun was now about its business. On the tops to the north, clear at last, the rain had fallen as snow; it brought them nearer and made them higher. The loch sparkled, the birches glittered, and the beeches shone. It was a day

of brisk and tinkling splendour. My stick tapped on the tarmac. I half expected to find the dairy beasts, which were
grazing below Tomdoun, wearing cowbells. A man waved
from the top of a ladder and a slate clattered on the roof. He
should have been yodelling.

I rounded a corner and there was Matilda sitting on the
grass verge and soaking up the sunshine. She was also panting.

'Hullo old girl. How goes it?'

Round the next bend were the rest of the cattle. They too
were strung along the verge, mostly sitting, and had the
resigned look of picketing strikers. Just above the road, and
commanding this peaceful scene, stood the little Tomdoun
hotel. The hotel *is* Tomdoun, and its gravel forecourt and
walls of dressed stone suggested a respectability we had not
seen since Broadford. The Land Rover was parked in the
forecourt and our three ponies were tethered to a verandah
whence they looked wistfully towards what might once have
been a croquet lawn. There was not a drover in sight. It must
be opening time.

In the bar a commercial traveller plied Julia with cokes; the
other drovers were on Bloody Marys. With only three miles to
go to the stance at Greenfield, and with a rest day scheduled
for tomorrow, the first pub for four days was doing a brisk
trade. Although it was cheering to think of the beasts waiting
patiently outside, all was not quite as it should be. Normally,
with shrubs and grass for the eating, they would have been up
and browsing. Upturn Brindle and Downturn Brindle should
have been locked in combat and Matilda lurking in the brambles as far from the gritty tarmac as she could get. They were
not cudding and they could hardly yet be tired. If they were
down it was because they wanted to get the weight off their
feet. Of all the possible dangers of which we had been warned
it was now clear that wear on the hooves was going to be the
major worry.

'We'd best start the formalin treatment right away. Morning and evening. There's beasts there that won't walk another

day on hard ground. And I'll need to get a good look at all
their feet. It may be that we'll have to rest some.'

Chris was as matter-of-fact as ever. He munched away at the
peanuts; he could have been passing judgement on the beer.
The rest of us were worried. Although an officer from the
SPCA had this morning congratulated us on the condition of
the beasts it was obvious to anyone who knew them well that
one or two were in some distress and that all were going to
elaborate lengths to avoid anything remotely hard. The coarse
chips used to surface minor roads and the abominable rock
confections favoured by the Hydro Board, plus the steep
gradients and the wet, had taken their toll. Even Jody had
sustained wear on her pads, especially her back feet, and
would henceforth require a daily anointing by the vet.

To be fair to the veterinary profession I must confess that
Chris had urged that the beasts be given a regular footbath
even before the drove started. Others had thought this an
unnecessary precaution and that the stress involved in administering it would not be commensurate with the benefits.
And anyway, how did one administer it? We had yet to find
anywhere that had a suitable walk-through trough; you
couldn't just splash the stuff in a puddle because it had to be
precisely diluted. It was also expensive and heavy and therefore had to be recoverable for subsequent baths.

Grasping the bull, as it were, by the hooves, Julia leapt from
her bar stool and made for the hotel telephone. She returned
triumphant. The Mothercare bath, in which small Keays had
lately splashed, was on its way. Gavin winced; but it was a
possibility. Alternatively she had in mind a black polypropy-
lene tank which could be borrowed from a trout-farming
friend. Next day, the rest day, Julia and I were intending to be
at home; I needed a morning on the telephone to make last-
minute arrangements with landowners and to adjust the route
in the light of what we had learned; we both needed a bath.
We would bring the fish tank back with us.

In the last resort there was a very different alternative

which, if the footbath failed, we would have to consider. In the old days it was common, though by no means invariable, practice to shoe drove cattle in much the same way as horses are shod. Appropriately enough, Invergarry, only a few miles down the glen from Tomdoun, is remembered as having a blacksmith who specialised in this work. But the practice seems only to have been widespread in the nineteenth century and there is no evidence of beasts from Skye having been shod before they reached Invergarry. The inference must then be that only after two or three days on one of Telford's roads – and with the prospect of further such roads ahead – was shoeing necessary.

'Keep their feet right and all will go well.' This was the advice of William McCombie, 'the grazier king', whose reputation as a cattle breeder was worldwide and who was largely responsible for the improvement of the Aberdeen-Angus breed in the mid-nineteenth century. Although based in Aberdeenshire, McCombie, and his father before him, bought cattle from all over the Highlands and Islands and their droves were invariably the sensation of the Falkirk tryst. Besides 'short stages and plenty of food' – plus drovers who were 'trained to their occupation' – the great secret was 'to have their feet properly dressed'.

> Everyone who has been in the cattle trade will recollect the losses he has sustained . . . by the animals throwing their hoofs; and we can all remember how often we have seen our beasts . . . lying on the roads, and how we had to cart them home or to the nearest slaughter house. If there be a separation of the hoof at the top from the skin, and if a white frothy substance oozes out at this break, it is a sure sign that irreparable injury has been done . . . The animal should be slaughtered immediately.

Fortunately it seemed that it was mainly in the spring and early summer that hooves were 'thrown'; in the autumn, if the weather was wet, the problem was that they wore down to the sensitive parts. In both cases McCombie stressed the importance of a pre-drove dressing and manicure.

9 When following a track the preferred formation was always single file to take advantage of the soft verge. JP and Chris in attendance

10 Below the Bealach (Pass of) Aoidhalean in Wester Ross

Before the time appointed for lifting the cattle, I sent across three or four able-bodied men who were acquainted with the dressing of the feet. Beginning their operations at the most northern part of the county, and going from one farm to another where cattle were wintered, they dressed every hoof of every bullock that required it. By dressing and by the proper training of the cattle before starting I have brought some thousands of them safe and sound.

Shoeing, on the other hand, was more restricted, only some beasts in each drove and only some feet on each beast being shod. The need for shoeing was only discovered after the beasts had been some days on the road. Haldane reports that droves from the north were often shod at Trinafour, south of the Drumochter pass, and those from the west at Tyndrum near Crianlarich – in other words, as they approached the skirts of the Highlands. Cattle from Wester Ross were shod at Muir of Ord where they joined the main east coast road and, from McCombie's comments, it would appear that those from the north-east were commonly shod at Perth. On one occasion the smithy there treated seventy cattle in a day which 'may appear incredible'. 'It should, however, be remembered that cattle, after being driven a distance, get more easily handled.' This was another good reason for delaying treatment.

Handling the beasts was indeed the real problem. In a byre you could run a rope from the rafters and haul up each leg in turn; 'this, however, must be a severe strain on the beasts'.

> The method I adopted when I was in the lean cattle trade was different; the bullock was driven to a wall; a man or two men secured him by the nose and the back of the neck. The fore feet were easy to hold up – one man could generally manage them; but the hind feet were not so easy a matter, and it always required two and sometimes three, strong men to hold them up. It is done entirely by method; not allowing the beast to stretch out his legs is the whole secret. The bullock has no power if his legs are kept close to his hind quarters; but if he is allowed to stretch them out he will throw off any number of men.

Allowing for a further man to nail on the shoes I made that six.

Probably it was just as common for the beasts to be simply thrown by roping their legs. If Hollywood is to be believed this was the normal method of subduing cattle in the Wild West and no doubt the same applied in Scotland. The notion that the stress this caused could have a harmful physiological effect seems not to have been generally appreciated.

At Invergarry, where the Skye cattle were probably shod, there is a tradition of wrestling with cattle which might be taken as corroboratory evidence. Under the patronage of Alister Ronaldson MacDonnell, one of the most irascible, belligerent and beloved of the clan chiefs, the MacDonnells held an annual gathering on an island in the Garry river. Joseph Mitchell, who seems to have attended it in about 1820, believed the Invergarry gathering to be the prototype of all the Highland Games which subsequently proliferated. There were the usual activities – 'dancing, piping, lifting a heavy stone, throwing the hammer, and running from the island to Invergarry and back, six miles'.

> The young men who ran came in exhausted and almost in a state of nudity for they had thrown off their kilts on the way and arrived in their shirts only. A blanket was cast over them and a glass of whisky administered.

But what really intrigued Mitchell was a novel field sport which seems to have been the only traditional event which lapsed as soon as Highland games figured on the social calendar.

> [This] was twisting the four legs from a cow, for which a fat sheep was offered as a prize. The cow was brought up and felled before the multitude, and the barbarous competition began, several men making the attempt. At last one man succeeded. After struggling for about an hour he managed to twist off the four legs and as a reward received his sheep with an eulogistic speech from the chief in Gaelic.

Throwing beasts, George had assured me, was not particularly difficult (hadn't he said the same thing about swimming?) although in the case of Highlanders there was a danger of damaging the horns. But first, where were we to obtain shoes and how were we going to fix them? A few have found their way into museums; they appear to have consisted of two crescent-shaped plates, one for each side of the cloven hoof, so eight per beast. They were attached with tacks but this must have been the most delicate operation since inside its nail-like hoof a cow's foot is more like a pad. And it was these pads that were already tender.

The more one went into it the more impossible it seemed – stressful for the beasts, distressing for the drovers and anathema to the SPCA. The footbath just had to work.

*   *   *

'Boy do we have trouble. You won't believe this . . .' Gavin was ringing from Tomdoun; it was going to be bad news. 'We've looked at nearly all of them. Feet have had it. Poor boys. The roads have knocked hell out of them. And get this. Their horns have gone floppy; you can just bend them, honestly. The bath? Oh come on, you must be joking. They just stepped over it. Frankly, John . . .'

I stopped listening. When Gavin starts a sentence with 'Frankly . . .' it means an ultimatum. Even allowing for exaggeration we had trouble enough. Julia and I loaded the fish tank and set off back to Glen Garry. Highland cattle are often described as having horns of a waxen character but this surely referred to their appearance, not their consistency. Of all the things that could go wrong with beasts under droving conditions, floppy horns was something no one had anticipated. The books said nothing about it and the Jeremiahs, though they had thought of everything else, had never hinted at it. It was cause for congratulation; we had managed to invent a new bovine malady.

Chris and Russell also vouched for it. In varying degrees all the horns were more bendy; they were also a bit flaky. JP could scarcely contain his delight; if they hadn't actually dropped off at least they'd be dangling by the time we reached

Crieff. But it was not all bad news. That there might be some connection between floppy horns and foot wear was something that occurred to all of us – calcium deficiency?

'I see,' said Chris. He had in fact already pursued this line of enquiry to its logical conclusion. The trouble must lie in their diet and the only food that they were getting that was not herbage was the cattle cobs. There must be something in the formulation of the cobs which was disturbing their natural balance. He was about to ring SAI and find out what it was.

If anyone deserved a quiet life it was Arthur Phillips, the Marketing Manager of Scottish Agricultural Industries. After a brief meeting and a single exchange of letters he had committed his company to supply us with feedstuffs, free, delivered and unlimited. He had asked for nothing in exchange and had never once attempted to interfere with or influence our arrangements. Yet he was far from indifferent to the drove. On Skye he had paid us a flying visit; to my shame I had failed to recognise him yet he had still dined us all at the Broadford Hotel. Subsequently he had somehow tracked us down at the god-forsaken bothy at Coireshubh. He arrived on an enormous motorbike, having ridden for four hours in torrential rain; he delivered veal stroganoff for seven cooked by his wife; and he then disappeared back into the monsoon. He was, in short, the epitome of a good sponsor.

When Chris broached the matter of the floppy horns his response was in keeping. The cattle cobs were a standard formulation except that, knowing the risk of staggers amongst beasts undergoing any kind of stress in the autumn months, his technical department had advised a double ration of magnesium. It was a typically solicitous and intelligent precaution and it was entirely our fault that no one had told him the cattle were getting the magnesium bullets anyway. As a result they were suffering from an overdose of magnesium. To redress the balance SAI would immediately make up a new formulation; they would deliver within 48 hours.

Encouraged by the thought that inexperienced droving was

not entirely to blame for the present crisis, we decided to try again with the footbath. The stance at Greenfield consisted of a field bisected by a track and entirely surrounded by forestry. The Forestry Commission's ranger lived in an adjacent house; otherwise it was a secluded spot. With the SPCA temporarily absent the moment was ripe for experimentation. This time we used the fish tank. It was filled to a depth of three inches with formalin solution and positioned at the narrow end of a small funnel contrived by using a gate, a hurdle and several fencing stobs.

The beasts were driven towards it, one person standing by the tank to check that all four feet of each beast went in and the rest massed behind. Twenty minutes of this produced scenes reminiscent of the swim. One or two inspected the tank and sniffed at the formalin, then turned and became wedged broadside across the outlet, so blocking it and causing the rest to mill around between them and us. Shoving and shouting was politely ignored. We cut out twelve at a time, then six at a time; it made no difference. Finally two of us got behind von Simpson and, ignoring the others, worked him into the outlet. He poked his head through above the solution but his horns were holding him back. It was the old problem, the one we had first encountered when trying to put them through the race at Oban. The price of having beasts with such superlative heads was that any race, crush or pen designed to keep them in single file was going to be too narrow for the spread of their horns. Since the tank was only two feet six inches wide the containing passage had to be the same. And since the boys invariably approached any such curiosity with their heads down they were bound to get stuck.

Having made his point and having satisfied himself that it was well taken, von Simpson tried again. This time we held back. He twisted his head through thirty degrees and with one horn forward like a rhino climbed slowly and deliberately into the tank. Desperately anxious not so much as to touch the woodwork he inched through. Before he was out at the other end, Downturn Brindle was queueing up to follow him. After a further half hour the whole lot were through and the precedent was set. We repeated the ritual the following morning and again in the evening. Thereafter it became routine. As confidence grew, the boys lifted their heads and we lowered the side posts; the most rudimentary funnelling arrangement sufficed.

As a chore it was more resented by the drovers than the driven. It meant humping twenty gallons of evil-smelling solution, finding a suitable wall or gate, and drawing on reserves of patience and humour that were often already exhausted. It was worth it if it worked, but as yet we could only hope.

10

'Along the sides of the mountains'

THE GREAT GLEN AND BEN NEVIS

After two days of heading west along Glen Garry we were now to lose a bit of latitude by heading south over the hills and down into the next east-west glen. Above the stance at Greenfield a high saddle breaks the line of rounded peaks. From a distance it looks as if it could be steep but in fact it is not; rather is it long, about eleven miles as the crow flies. First you climb by gently sloping tracks through a well-grown forest of larch and spruce. You emerge onto a desolate incline, bounded on either side by distant ridges and devoid even of footpaths. The watershed is near the top of this plane and, soon after, the craggy mass of Meall an Tagraidh barges in from the west to hustle the little Cia-aig burn into the glen of the same name. The glen quickly grows tighter and steeper as it disappears under a dense canopy of mature forestry. At the bottom is the so-called Dark Mile with its road tunnelling through the trees between Lochs Arkaig and Lochy. This is the entrance to the Great Glen, our half-way point.

Eleven miles is not an unreasonable distance for cattle already used to droving conditions and we had originally planned to cross this long shoulder in one day. Now, concern for the state of the cattle, plus the delays of footbathing, put it out of the question. Instead we moved the beasts up to the top of the Glen Garry forestry on the first day, held them there overnight in the electric fence with Russell staying as nightwatchman, and tackled the bald uplands and Glen Cia-aig on the following day.

This was the route over which Thomas Telford had proposed building a new road in order to cut the corner involved in
following the Garry down to Invergarry. The road had never
materialised but – or perhaps *therefore* – what he called this
'mountain pass' remained a popular droving route throughout
the nineteenth century. Near the watershed, at a ruined bothy
called Fedden, there was even a recognised stance. Why a
stance was needed in such a desolate place or why the droves
habitually broke journey after just six miles from Glen Garry
was something of a mystery. It could be that at this stage of the
journey they, like us, were seeing the first signs of possible
deterioration in the cattle and decided therefore to take it easy.
Thanks to generations of droving traffic, Fedden's few acres
of flat ground had, and still have, a bloom of green, the result
of treading and manuring. If it hadn't been for the impossibility of carrying the fish tank and the formalin to such a remote
spot, we too would have preferred to stop there rather than at
the top of the forest road.

But as we inched towards the watershed another explanation came to mind. In a straight line we were averaging less
than one mile per hour and it was hard to see how, even by
making more use of the dogs, this could be improved on. The
bit of knotted string which I used for calculating distances on
the map had already acquired a certain notoriety. Contrary to
general belief it was not elastic, nor had it shrunk; but on
ground like this I had to admit that it could give a misleading
impression of the distance actually to be covered.

Scouting ahead to find the most promising line up to the
watershed I turned to bellow directions and found that I was
already too far ahead. Gavin's dogs had the beasts in a tight
bunch but the ground was perilously soft and they were having to make wide sweeps from one small knoll to the next.
Behind them the greens and golds of Glen Garry had now
slipped below the immediate horizon. In their place a sterner
panorama of mountain and moor had tilted into view. It
stretched away an impossible distance into the far north. As

opposed to the choppy hills along the sea-board of Wester Ross we were now on the heavy swell of the Highlands proper. White and ghostly the peaks of Kintail and Glen Affric scraped the clouds; more snow was on the way and the probability must now be that it would lie all winter. Even without the snow the scene would have served to emphasise the emptiness of the Highlands. Threading the glens and following the roads one gets a totally misleading impression of verdure and cultivation. Up here lay the reality; mile upon mile of desolate hill and virgin moorland, without a tree or a pylon, devoid for most of the year of colour and character, magnificent and now indeed precious, but also intimidating and immensely depressing. To venture across this heaving wilderness, whether for shooting deer, gathering sheep, or droving cattle, could only be effrontery. Tightly packed and proof against the foulest weather, thirty head of Highland cattle here counted for no more than a cluster of plankton tossing in a wave-trough.

The floor of this particular trough was a dreary expanse of peat. Somewhere in the middle of it a lochan marked the watershed; the general impression was that of continuous moor rather than of 'a mountain pass'. Glacier-like, the peat was cut about with crevasses and banks that oozed a black and oily tea. So bad were these hags that Gavin, who had previously tried to find a path through them, had written off this whole section as impossible. Subsequent enquiries had revealed that the old track did not follow the floor of the glen at all but contoured round the high ground that formed its western boundary. This was where the cattle were now picking their way with one man below to ensure that they kept well above the peat flats. It reminded me of a sentence in one of Lieutenant Burt's letters. 'I have several times seen them driving great numbers of cattle along the sides of the mountains at a great distance but never, except once, was near them.' (The 'once' was when he saw them swimming a river 'like spaniels' while the drovers gave voice with their 'hideous cry'.) This observation from a man who travelled extensively, especially in Inverness-shire, during the early eighteenth century is in marked contrast to those of nineteenth-century travellers who invariably encountered their droves on or near a road.

Many upland glens, especially near a watershed, are similar to the one leading to Fedden in that the floor is far too soft for cattle. Moreover, in happier times, the floors even of lowland glens would have been equally out of bounds, all level ground being appropriated for growing the food on which the then considerable population depended. It is often said of the Highlands that wherever rushes now grow there once was arable and wherever bracken now grows there once was the best pasture. If this was the case, cattle and drovers would seldom have come off 'the sides of mountains'.

Working their way along the hill our boys habitually adopted a loose formation more like the 'bow' than the 'column' but dictated entirely by the lie of hollows and rocky outcrops. The pattern left on mud, say, or snow would have been of up to a dozen more or less parallel tracks across the face of the hill occasionally coming together in just one or two streams where a burn had to be crossed or a pocket of bog skirted. In glens where neither new roads nor new fences have disturbed the natural flowlines I sometimes thought I could detect bands of leached stones or of greener pasturage where the cattle would naturally have walked. In this trough leading up to Fedden and again in the glen from Lairig Leacach down to Loch Treig such bands were unmistakable. But a hundred years of growth and decay, of frost, drought and downpour may well have erased all trace of the droves. Perhaps it was the work of deer and sheep that I was seeing.

The only problem with hillsides was that they considerably lengthened the day's journey. Instead of walking in a straight line we were looping in and out of each fold in the hills. And since the ground was usually broken, the beasts could not be hurried.

'But I've got to push, I've got to push.' Gavin sounded like an expectant mother in the last stages of labour. I resisted. We were 'taking our piece' just short of Fedden; that meant we had done four miles in five hours. There was rather more to come. But the beasts looked happy to be off the roads; the Brindle frères were locked in combat, and the ponies were still out of sight behind us.

'Piece' in Gavin's case was again proving a misnomer; a whole loaf of wholemeal came out of one pocket and full jars of peanut butter and marmite out of the other.

'You should never go on the hill without taking at least twenty-four hours' food. You know that. Standard practice for heaven's sake. Compass, waterproofs, matches and a day's food.'

But the day's food was not getting a chance to last the day and hence, no doubt, the sense of urgency. To put his mind at rest, but mainly to save the beasts, I volunteered to shorten the day's walk. Instead of the long descent through forestry to the Dark Mile we would stop as soon as we reached a forest track with a turning place suitable for a large lorry. The large lorry in question was a cattle transporter. We were about to cheat.

Leaving Gavin to bring on the cattle I went ahead to arrange the rendezvous. In the depths of the forest above the Dark Mile a small new car appeared. This was Lochiel country and in the car was Lochiel himself. We were a day late and he had come to look for us. The field was ready. Would we like baths? The drove was going jolly well, wasn't it? A meal perhaps?

I declined. It was not that I feared the Cameron stricture – 'You grow effeminate, sir' – but that we were about to speed off in the lorry. He could not have appeared at a more embarrassing moment.

'That's extremely kind, sir. The trouble is that we have to press on. We're already a day late but we're trying to catch up.'

'Got the lorry lined up have you?'

How did he know? I had completely forgotten that three months ago it was actually he who had recommended trucking the beasts across the Great Glen. At that time we were haunted by the carnage that could result from a traffic accident. Between the Dark Mile and Corriechoillie (Roy Bridge) there was no way of avoiding a whole day on the public highway including a mile or two on the main Fort William to Inverness road through Spean Bridge. This was before we had discovered that cattle had as much right on the roads as cars and before the Inverness constabulary had offered a police escort. In all honesty that excuse no longer held.

But it was still true that there was nothing to be learnt from eight miles on trunk roads and, with the cattle's feet in such a parlous state, there was much at risk. If the gravel surface of Telford's roads had been 'injurious to the hoofs' how much more so were the granite chips embedded in the unyielding tarmac of the A82 and the B8004. As always the cattle must come first.

Appropriately the cattle transporter belonged to a local haulage contractor called Bowman. The driver was unable to confirm whether his boss's family had always been in the business of moving cattle and the suited gentleman who was also in the cab was not a Bowman at all but an SAI sales representative. He had just crashed his car – it lay a crumpled wreck in a ditch near Gairlochy – but the new cattle cobs were safe. He had rushed them from a factory at the other end of Scotland and was now perched on top of them. The label read 'Drove Cobs'; he guaranteed they contained no magnesium.

Two miles up into the forestry Gavin and the drove were waiting. There was still no sign of the ponies or their handlers which meant that the two of us would have to load the beasts. Without a loading bay this could be a taxing operation. The dogs, the driver, and the sales rep all showed willing, but it was Matilda who took the initiative. We should have known that she could be counted on to recognise a soft option. With Gavin and fifteen of the heavier beasts she was trundled away down the forest road while I waited with the remainder – and in due course the ponies – for the second shuttle.

Already the light was fading. The wind sighed in the tree tops and stags roared up the glen. It was October 22nd; the stags were at last safe till next year – and we were half-way to Crieff. If one allowed for the extra time spent on Skye it was more like two-thirds. But ahead lay the dreaded 'empty quarter' consisting of the highest section of the route (round Ben Nevis) and the most exposed (across Rannoch Moor). At anywhere over 1,000 feet in the West and Central Highlands late October blizzards are not uncommon. Bad weather, discomforting in the coastal glens, could there be disastrous. And bad weather did indeed seem to be our lot. October is traditionally one of the stormiest months of the year and, in many places, October '81 would be the wettest and windiest on record.

Against this must be set our growing confidence in handling the cattle. Under normal conditions, and drawing on inexhaustible stores of patience, we could take them almost anywhere. Matilda still strayed, though never far, and Gavin (the beast, not the drover) still held back to snatch a mouthful of whatever was going. But there was a real sense of cohesion. Walking with a favourite dog one soon acquires a sixth sense as to its whereabouts; and so it was with the cattle. We still counted them through every gate but the count was now a formality. One *felt* that one was missing, sensed that something was amiss, long before the problem was identified.

'They're looking well,' said Lochiel; and if one knew nothing about their floppy horns and caught them on soft ground they did look well. But having seen them on rock and gravel, and having inspected the state of their feet, we now knew that lameness, rather than weather or terrain, was going to be the decisive factor.

*   *   *

To Lochiel I am indebted for an undated pamphlet about the most famous of all Highland drovers and one of the few of whom anything is known. The author of the pamphlet is Alastair Cameron and the subject John Cameron (1780–1856), otherwise known as 'Corry' or 'Corriechoillie' after the name of his home (and our next stance) near Roy Bridge. Corry's career neatly illustrates the extremes of situation and fortune to be found amongst those who became drovers. He was born near Spean Bridge, the great bottle-neck for all the droves from the north-west, and he made his first pennies minding beasts while their drovers were getting a dram in the nearby inn. His father was either the innkeeper (according to Alastair Cameron) or a poor crofter (according to Joseph Mitchell). Either way he died young leaving Corry with a few goats and nothing else. The boy sold the goats, hired himself out as a drover's lad, and set off barefoot for his first visit to the Falkirk tryst.

With wages thus earned he bought the odd stirk and started dealing profitably on his own account. In due course he rented a farm off Lochiel and dealt in sheep as well. Soon he had his own droves. He rented more farms, bought more stock and continued to prosper. But he remained a dealer and drover rather than a farmer or breeder. Whilst consolidating his holdings in Lochaber he also leased ground as far away as Crieff and Loch Tayside. In his heyday it was said that when he bought cattle on Skye he could rest them on his own grass every night of the way to Falkirk. At a time when land was rapidly being enclosed for sheep and when drovers were being charged for every bite of grazing, this was a mighty advantage. He was also in a position to extend the same facilities – for a fee – to other drovers. No one can have appreciated more than we how much this must have simplified matters. In effect what he was trying to do was to establish a monopoly of the north-west droving trade.

Like most dealers he seems to have been a volatile figure having more of the punter's nervous energy than of the far- mer's solid endeavour. Short, thin, 'with a sharp hooked nose and lynx eyes', he was invariably badly dressed and short of sleep. According to Mitchell, 'he frequently rode night and day on a wiry pony from Falkirk to the Muir of Ord (the main tryst in the north), 120 miles, carrying for himself some bread and cheese in his pocket and giving his pony now and then a bottle of porter.' It was part of his legend to be both everywhere and nowhere. He would claim that never once in fifty years had he missed the three sales of the Falkirk tryst yet he moved so fast and dressed so disreputably that he often went unnoticed.

In the telling, his life has become a series of anecdotes. There is the one about the young gentleman on the Fort William to Glasgow steamer who sees a disreputable old crofter casting an impertinent eye over his blushing young bride. Rather than admonish him the young gentleman prefers to make him a laughing stock and offers to sell him his wife for £1,000. Of course, 'the old fool' is Corriechoillie. He slips off the ship when it calls at Greenock, dashes to the bank, and is there on the quayside waving a thousand crisp notes when the ship docks in Glasgow. The gentleman protests it was only a joke; Corry insists that a deal is a deal; and the poor girl no doubt swoons. Eventually Corry relents; he will drop his case if the gent will stand his employees a dinner at the Eagle Hotel. Still unaware of the crofter's identity the gent agrees and on the appointed day some fifty assorted shepherds, stockmen and drovers descend on the hotel consuming £100-worth of champagne and roasts.

Mitchell's story of Corry's appearance at the Court of Sessions is equally revealing of the man's mischievous nature. It is also perhaps a more typical specimen of Highland anecdote. Corry had been summoned as a witness in some dispute concerning how many sheep a particular farm could support. As usual he was dressed like a pauper and counsel therefore presumed, in the most patronising manner, to enquire into his credentials.

'Do you know anything about sheep?'
'Aye, a little.'

'How many sheep have you got?'
'I am not sure.'
'Have you got 100?'
'Och yes.'
'Have you got 500?'
'Och yes.'
'How many have you then?'
'I canna be sure.'
'Have you 5,000?'
'Och yes, I heave.'
'How many have you?'
'I am not sure.'
'Well, have you 20,000?'
'I am thinking I heave more.'
'Have you 40,000?'
'Och yes.'
'How many have you?'
'Weel, I canna be sure.'
'Have you 50,000?'
'Och yes'

And so on. The story depends on a slow delivery and a subtly different tone of response to each question. There is no punchline. Like one of Corry's vast droves, it just keeps on flowing past until the point is taken.

By the 1840s Corry was reputedly the largest leaseholder in Scotland and was reckoned to own more stock than any man in the British Isles. If pressed, he admitted that on the world scene it was possible that Prince Esterhazy had more – but that man had an unfair advantage in that he paid no rent for his grazings. Corry's combined stock of cattle and sheep would at any given time certainly have been in six figures.

To some extent success was no doubt the result of shrewd dealing and a good eye for a carcase. But he also attempted to outwit and manipulate the market. A near monopoly of some drove routes helped. Additionally he seems, like many dealers and farmers today (including our Oban patron, Hughie), to have appreciated the need to hold stock back when prices were low or the stock in less than peak condition. Animals bought in the spring would be summered on his grazings in Lochaber and others wintered on the low ground in Perthshire.

11 Russell and Julia attempt to coax the ponies onto an ice-glazed bridge near
Loch Eilde Mor, Invernesshire

12 Forsaking so-called drove roads, the cattle take to the tops on the decisive day above Blackwater. The peaks behind are those of Glen Coe

To what extent this practice was common amongst other dealer/drovers it is impossible to say. But it may well be that as many as half of the cattle that left Skye every year were not driven straight to the Falkirk tryst at all. For every description of drove beasts in peak condition there is another where they are described as a pitiful sight, small, ill-formed and under-nourished. Such cattle were in no condition to be driven vast distances let alone sold. The speciality of the Highlands and Islands was not the production of fatstock but breeding and rearing. 'Lowland' or 'English beef on Highland bone' was the cry.

Today there is almost as much movement of stock between grazings as there is between markets. Sheep and cattle may be shunted from one end of the Highlands to the other to take advantage of lush summer or winter grass. From the hills of Argyll hoggs (year-old ewes) are sent to the Black Isle (no blacker than 'black' houses or 'black' cattle) of Cromarty or to Perthshire for wintering. Just above Corriechoillie – the place, that is – we met, and made way for, a drove of sheep coming down to Roy Bridge for transport to Caithness. In the hard accents of the north-east the shepherd explained that he took the high grazing below Ben Nevis to summer his flock while the grass recovered on his Caithness farm.

Probably he had planted a few acres of turnips which would also help to see them through the Caithness winter. The better use of grazing and the value of winter feeding like turnips was first exploited in the early nineteenth century by the likes of William McCombie, 'the grazier king' of Aberdeenshire; and it was there and throughout the north-east that this style of farming flourished. When McCombie bought cattle on Skye it was not to drive them straight down to Falkirk but to bring them over to Morayshire or Aberdeenshire for wintering and a chance of cashing in on higher prices in the following spring and early summer. Similarly Corry owed much of his success to 'bringing on' in Lochaber stock bought cheaply in the spring in Skye and elsewhere and to wintering stock on his Perthshire holdings. The notion that all Highland droving took place in the autumn and that it consisted of a headlong dash from the local markets to the Crieff or Falkirk trysts is a wild over-simplification. Like the received idea that the cattle were all black, the drovers all romantically clad Landseer look-alikes, and their trails all well-defined and neatly turfed 'drove roads', it needed heavy qualification.

According to Joseph Mitchell, Corry 'did not die a rich man'. Although he has the distinction, rare indeed, of having made a fortune in the Highlands he also managed to lose it there – a far commoner occurrence. It seems that his capital was always tied up in stock, not land; he never bought an acre. Higher rents, a few lean years and a few incautious deals were enough to work off any surplus profits. He continued to trade until, at the age of seventy-five, while doing the rounds of his stock, the wiry little man on the wiry little horse collapsed. He is buried at Roy Bridge.

At the height of his fame it is said that Corry's Falkirk drove stretched all the way from his home at Corriechoillie to Lairig Leacach. Besides being proof that this little-frequented glen round the back of Ben Nevis was an authentic drove route, this span happened to be precisely the distance we covered on October 23rd. Not that that gave any clue as to how many beasts such a drove might have contained. Local tradition has it that Corriechoillie farm in the nineteenth century was con-siderably to the south of its present position in what is now an impenetrable forest. There is also no way of knowing just how closely such a vast drove might have been packed or what percentage of the animals were sheep. With large droves of cattle the custom seems to have been to divide them into manageable groups or 'bows'. 'The second division follows the first,' related one witness, 'they are kept apart from one another by their drovers.'

To confuse matters further none of us could agree on how far we had actually travelled that day. It was my turn for the

Land Rover and I made it a mere five miles. JP, who walked it, said it was at least seven, all uphill. His description of the day's events had a predictable flavour. During the footbath routine two bystanders had got doused with formalin ('they didn't feel a thing; they were journalists'). Then the beasts had 'escaped' into an unthinned plantation of sitka spruce ('it was like a Neanderthal mammoth hunt; we careered through the trees bent double, hands trailing on the ground'). Next our heroic brownie was kicked on the shin by a bony yellow beast. It emerged that this was not the first time this had happened; nor would it be the last (I believe he was the only drover that ever got kicked; he swears that it was always the same beast). The Caithness shepherd, whom the rest of us found both interested and informative, had greeted JP with the news that all our cattle were about to die 'and then merrily went on his way'. It had also rained non-stop.

From this description of a fairly average day I concluded that our brownie was in good heart again. The same could not be said for the cattle. So far the formalin treatment had had no apparent effect and there was scarcely a beast that was not feeling its feet. To walk behind them was no longer a cheering experience. One winced with every patch of stones and groaned with every slab of rock. The quality of the going had become an obsession. Just as the cyclist finds steep what the motorist never notices so the drover finds excruciating what the walker takes in his stride. Never has the surface of Highland tracks been so carefully studied. We were becoming connoisseurs of pebbles and shingle, experts on chips and gravel, geological know-alls about moraines and rock. Hand-laid, man-made, unmade, each dotted track on the map had its distinctive character.

Perhaps the ground would have become less of a preoccupation had there been other things to see. But the cloud was down, the rain relentless. On the way up to Lairig Leacach the track followed a demented burn which even when out of sight was never out of hearing. From a distance it boomed with a steady thunder; closer to, the thunder, which may have been caused by the shunting of boulders along its bed, was drowned out by the crashing and hissing of white water. A fine spray rose from each waterfall and tongues of foaming current flicked up from the centre of the flood. Hurtling down its rock-strewn gully it had a savage and uncompromising character that was in keeping with how I imagined the setting.

At the Lairig Leacach bothy the cloud lifted and the rain stopped just long enough for the luxury of an alfresco shave. I sat on a rock with a towel and a mug of hot water relishing the release from cumbrous waterproofs. We were – and evidently had been for most of the day – in a long glen so narrow and wet and deep that it was like those pictures of the Red Sea with its waters penned back to make a passage for the Israelites. For 2,000 feet on either side the walls of the glen soared upwards. In places they were cut about by sheer rock faces with cascades of boulders perilously suspended beneath. Elsewhere the slopes were vertically corrugated as if to give added strength to support whatever lay over the skyline. The map showed peaks of 3,500 feet on both sides but even on the clearest day their smile can hardly bring cheer into this trench-like glen. The bare stone of the bothy glistened with damp and blended into the streaming cliffs behind.

Next day the cloud was back and, as we climbed still higher, it crept in below as well as above. We were now working round the eastern edge of the Grey Corries, a spur of ridges and peaks radiating from Aonach Beag and Ben Nevis. From what one could see of it, it was not cattle country. The heather grew shorter and woodier. It offered no grazing and was hardly kinder to tender feet than the crags it carpeted. Increasingly the tap of unshod hoof on bare rock broke the silence of altitude. In place of the yellows and browns of autumn we were in a wintry world of black and white in which cloud-light shone from bare and glistening slabs of rock where the black heather could gain no purchase. In the wet even the russets and golds of the cattle had turned a tawny grey. The beasts looked taller and more angular, creatures of horn and bone for a landscape of rock and stone.

When the slabs of rock levelled back into a path and swung left past a scattering of cairns we halted. It must be the top of the pass; we were at 2,000 feet, the highest point so far. Cloud billowed above, below and around. In spite of the cold wind the ponies were steaming. And for once the sound of rushing water was stilled. With the silence came that sense of liberation so special to high places. For an instant the sun almost broke through; then it changed its mind. Instead a rent in the cloud revealed a wall of rock where the sky should be. It was topped with snow like a slice of birthday cake.

'Is that Ben Nevis?'

'No. Must be the Grey Corries. You can't see the Ben from here. It's behind.'

Behind, above, below, it made no difference. Under present conditions everything was just billowing cloud and one felt like hanging on to the ground for reassurance. We finished the chocolate bars, stoppered the bottles, and plunged down in search of scenery and softer going.

Originally the plan had been to take the next glen east and miss out on this pass altogether. That would have taken us down to Loch Treig and thence to Blackwater. But it meant two, possibly three, days out of reach of the Land Rover, and with the cattle in their present condition that seemed too risky. Our expectations of further progress now stretched no further than the next night's stance. We had to be certain that at each and every halt we could transport cattle out. Obviously there were no roads suitable for lorries but if there was a track that a Land Rover could manage then, in emergency, we could bring in the trailer. It would be exaggerating to say that we expected to move the whole drove in this way but at least we could take out the odd beast. We could then limp on to the main road at Kingshouse, three days from Lairig Leacach, and there decide whether to abort the whole project. Increasingly this was looking like a probability.

The new route promised a motorable track by the end of the day which could thereafter be followed all the way to Blackwater. But first it had the disadvantage of the pass, and then of a river. According to a bearded Yorkshireman who had temporarily attached himself to the drove and who seemed to have spent most of his life tramping through the Highlands, the river should be possible as long as it was not in spate. He called it 'the old Abhainn Rath', confidently enunciating the Gaelic as if it were a West Riding patois. He spoke about it with such feeling and familiarity that, when finally poised on its grassy banks, we sized it up with exaggerated respect, spread left and right in search of a possible ford, and argued the pros and cons of each possible line.

It was not now in spate but it would have been yesterday. All the short burns and rivers running off the Ben Nevis chain are highly volatile, rising to enormous heights in the space of an hour or two and falling just as rapidly. The Abhainn Rath drains the south face of the Grey Corries and after just eight miles empties into Loch Treig. Where we were crossing it at Luibeilt, three miles above the loch, it was about thirty feet wide, very fast, and the bottom strewn with loose stones. But it had already dropped by a couple of feet and it was still dropping. The boys played along with the sense of occasion, shying away and mooing in protest; they always exploited uncertainty. But once in the water they knew well enough that it was only belly deep and nothing out of the ordinary. Von Simpson and the Brindles calmly took a diagonal to the best landing place on the other side; the rest followed in their own good time. Matilda swished her tail by way of a tut-tut over the loose stones and Ickle Brindle had to tread water for a moment when he lost his footing. As so often, it was the discomfort and uncertainty of the footing which worried them, not the current or depth of the water.

At Corriechoillie Chris had taken out two beasts; one had severe wear on the back of its hooves – its heels as it were – and the other had worn the protective membrane on its soles to a wafer-thin fragility. Today Russell was taking them down to Argyll in the trailer and already it was apparent that at least one, probably two, were ready to follow. The sooner we got them out the quicker their feet would recover and the sooner they would be able to rejoin the drove. But at what point did one have to call a halt? Shunting beasts back and forth was exhausting work. The trailer had to be emptied of two tons of feedstuffs, fencing materials etc.; the beasts had to be cut out, coaxed in, cautiously driven and unloaded; then the trailer had to be washed out, driven back and reloaded with the feedstuffs. Additionally, and perhaps more to the point, if this sort of thing went on, if the drove began to look appreciably smaller, someone was going to start asking embarrassing questions.

For the final stage of the day's journey I walked with the ponies. We were still over 1,000 feet but the cloud had cleared and to the south the hills were beginning to open out towards Rannoch Moor. Two more ridges, one each side of the Blackwater reservoir, and we would be on the flat. From the Eilde lochs, where we proposed to spend the night, the track took a long loop round the first ridge and then zig-zagged above the river Leven up to the dam. None of us knew the ground; from the map it looked like two days' work over steep and probably rocky terrain. The only alternative was to charge straight over the ridge. Although neither on the map nor on the ground was there any sign of a track, the contours looked possible. I left Julia to bring on the ponies and went ahead to make a reconnaissance.

The problem with all the drove routes south from Lairig Leacach – and there are several, some heading for the Rannoch side of the moor and others for the Glen Coe side – is the Blackwater reservoir which provides power for the aluminium smelter at Kinlochleven. Lying east–west and about ten miles long, this arm of lifeless water now effectively blocks all routes. The only way round is below the dam at the west end or miles to the east by way of Lochs Ossian and Rannoch.

There was therefore no question here of following an authentic route. We were improvising and if improvisation was the name of the game the short cut over the ridge looked fine. It was soft, dangerously soft in places, but even a bog was better than stones.

I crossed the ridge and cantilevered out above the gorge of the Leven until the dam was in sight. Then I turned back. To walk without either tugging at a pony or dawdling at a cow's pace was wonderfully exhilarating. To the west the last of the sun glanced off the Mamore hills. Below I could just make out the cattle gratefully fanning out on the grass beside Loch Eilde Beag. The contrast between the menacing Blackwater with its bleached shoreline and these placid pools was the difference between a salt lake and the village pond. The beasts grazed at the water's edge, and a fringe of reeds where a narrow channel connected the two lochs hinted at sea trout and dragonflies. Smoke was now rising from the tin shed that had been appropriated as the cookhouse. A small tent was going up. The Land Rover was slowly crawling along the glen from Kinlochleven.

The place was remote enough to suggest a challenge to Arthur Phillips. In scarlet gaiters and natty waterproofs SAI's Marketing Manager strode into camp just as a hailstorm ended the day. The twelve-mile walk with Mrs P.'s dinner-for-seven in a backpack deserved more than the weary thanks it got as we downed spare-ribs and chianti in the squalidest hut imaginable.

In the night it froze; day broke with dense fog. When the boys loomed out of the murk to set about breakfast their tails, fringes and forelocks were braided with ice. Chris singled out two more beasts for examination and using fence-posts, ropes and sweet-talk we somehow managed to get a look at their hind feet. The technique was not quite as McCombie recommended but he would have approved the decision to rest them both. That meant getting the trailer up, a daunting task for which only Russell, the owner, could take responsibility. I volunteered to help him. Today, if any day, would decide whether or not we went on to Crieff. If with soft going the beasts continued uncomfortable, that was it. I wanted to know the outcome, but not to experience ten hours of agonising over it.

11

'An ocean of blackness and bogs'

THE MOOR OF RANNOCH

'OK. How'd it go?' Gavin, JP and the beasts had reached Blackwater first – a good sign?

'Piece of cake. Luckily they didn't let any water out when we were under the dam. I bet you didn't warn them. God, what a fabulous day. You could see right to . . .'

'No, you ass, the beasts. How'd they do?'

'Great. No problems.'

'I mean their feet.'

'Never felt them. That bitch Matilda was up to her tricks. Got on a rock in the middle of the river and wouldn't come off. JP had to go in after her.'

'But no sign of lameness?' It was hardly credible. Could the problem have just vanished? The formalin must be working.

'Well it was soft, wasn't it? By the way, steer clear of Julia. She didn't appreciate your short cut. They've had a helluva day with the ponies.'

Preoccupied with the state of the cattle we had been taking the ponies for granted. Their problems had usually been dismissed as of a minor order. There had been the laminitis scare on Skye and in Glen Garry the grey, Rona, had developed a mysterious swelling that looked like mumps. Chris had said 'I see' and successfully treated it. Fit from a summer's trekking and specially shod for the drove they had taken both the rough and the smooth in their sturdy stride. Only on peat had they caused a few scares – just enough to suggest that the soft going which the cattle craved was not their ideal.

The first problem, however, had been of a different order. To get started that morning the whole drove had had to cross the small but deep burn which linked Loch Eilde Beag with Loch Eilde Mor. Surprisingly in such a remote glen there was a small foot-bridge. It was old, narrow and rickety; it was also covered in ice. In the absence of sand, Russell took it into his head to treat the ice with oatmeal. This could have been a brilliant expedient had it continued to freeze. But at that moment the sun appeared and, as the veils of mist began to trail away up the hillsides, the oatmeal congealed into slimy porridge. The ponies sniffed it and backed away. They wouldn't cross; they wouldn't even lick their way along it. With tackety boots slithering in all directions Russell hauled at Eilidh, the bay, from in front while Julia laid into her rump with the only whip to hand, a none too persuasive woollen scarf. This went on for some minutes and was much enjoyed by all who watched. Eventually Eilidh sprang forward and, landing in the porridge, appeared to do the splits. As so often it could have been disastrous. But she recovered. Once she was across Rona and Mhari followed in less impetuous style. Meanwhile, just upstream, the cattle lowered themselves into the water one by one, swam a few nonchalant strokes and set off up the hill. It was a hint of things to come.

Having saddled and loaded up, Julia returned to help pack up the camp confident of being able to overtake the beasts. While her back was turned Eilidh and Mhari had a minor tiff which soon became a kicking match. Julia's diary takes up the story.

Dashed back to sort them out but arrived to find Mhari with a snapped buckle on her head-collar and Eilidh with a broken girth. Unload their packs – find new girth and spare head-collar – put them on – reload packs. Decide to get under way immediately. Chris and Liz, the other Orkney vet (how many vets are there on the Orkneys?) each take a pony. Just over the first rise Rona slips, falls awkwardly and breaks another girth. Congratulations on having yet another 'spare' cut short by realisation that it's in one of Mhari's panniers and underneath the veterinary gear. Unload fifty assorted bottles, jars, kidney bowls etc., unsaddle, regirth, re-saddle, repack.

Still a dazzling morning. Sun actually warm, snowline receding, but we can still follow the tracks of the cattle because their thick-coated legs have brushed the rime from the grass – looks like someone's been dragging a dinosaur across the hill. First signs of peat just over the top – great black sinister gashes with an evil glitter of water at the bottom. Skirt round on what seems like a firm crust. Keeping Eilidh behind I stamp with each step and, every fourth, jump with heels down. No give. Feel faintly ridiculous. Then, mid-hopscotch, am brought up short. Eilidh has stopped. It can't be. She has a sixth sense about peat. But it can. All four legs are through the crust and into the peat. She's stuck up to her belly, unable to move.

Keep calm – a chance to show your mettle in a crisis. But, dear God, she's going to break a leg. That's when they shoot them. Even two vets can't save a horse with a broken leg. I shriek at the others to get back but they're already on the peat. We all freeze, figures in a landscape, marooned in time. Do I pull on the leading rope? Unsaddle? What do I do? She mustn't panic. The others can't help; they have to keep Rona and Mhari away. But Chris is smiling. 'She'll manage' he shouts and turns Rona away. Am about to explode with rage when Eilidh proves him right. Dear, crotchety, independent old Eilidh is struggling and lurching and gradually working her legs free.

The next ninety minutes will haunt me forever. We were fifty yards onto the crust with fifty yards to go. We prodded the ground, backed and circled. But Rona's forelegs went through, then Eilidh's again and finally it was Mhari's turn. Weighed down by the panniers she went in even deeper than Eilidh. But the panniers were also her saving. They stuck on the surface like buoyancy tanks and held her up. Chris was wonderful. His calm steadied them, steadied me. At last, with a frantic, grunting scramble, we were out.

How marvellous to be born placid. Like the cattle, Chris plonked himself down and unconcernedly started munching a cheese sandwich. I hared round looking for the next hazard and hunting for the tracks of the cattle. We were almost on top of them. Where we had floundered and staggered and sunk they had trotted happily across. How dare they?

That night we sat out under the stars round a roaring fire. Save for the distant peaks above Glen Coe the hills were gentler here and the Blackwater reservoir stretched away to the east with a flat and irregular shoreline. It felt higher than it was; even the stars seemed brighter and clearer. The tents, pitched near the southern end of the dam and somewhat above it, were sheltered by a couple of abandoned cottages from the cruel breeze that funnelled up Glen Leven. Presumably they had been built to house workers on the dam. Rusting chunks of machinery and wasted lumps of concrete protruded from the peat – yesterday's industrial scrap, tomorrow's archaeological artefacts. Even our firewood was mostly old building timber.

But if not the most romantic setting, it was the first entirely relaxed evening in three weeks. The beasts were on the mend, the ponies had survived their severest test, it was Liz's birthday, and for a whole day it had not rained. The grass glittered with frost and sparks from the fire exploded into the sky to chase the shooting stars. We lay out late savouring the brittle night and relishing the camaraderie – a little pool of warmth and euphoria in the black silence of the hills. I remember only an enduring sense of privilege.

*   *   *

Although the West Highlands and the Islands are still the main breeding ground of Highland cattle there are numerous folds elsewhere in the British Isles and several in North America, Germany and Scandinavia. Increasingly buyers from overseas are showing a keen interest in the Highlander's peculiar ability to forage for its food on marginal and hill ground and to survive the most adverse conditions. The Highland Cattle Society is dedicated to emphasising this commercial value; whilst they cannot but recognise that the breed owes its survival largely to its endearing and decorative appeal, they contend, with good reason, that it still has a role in beef production. The meat of Highlanders is lean and of exceptional quality. The beasts are also cross-bred with other breeds to produce crosses of great commercial value.

If any evidence of the animals' hardiness, ability to survive on almost anything, and general docility were needed the droving tradition offers a powerful testimony. But in Canada experiments have recently been conducted to establish the breed's suitability for the semi-arctic conditions of Alberta. It was tested, along with three other breeds, to discover the lowest temperature at which each would continue to thrive and produce offspring without diverting its energy to sustaining body-heat. With a critical temperature of minus 40°C the North American bison was the runaway winner. But the Highlander, at minus 16–20°C, came an equal and creditable second with the Himalayan yak; the Hereford, 'the most popular breed in the world', trailed a poor fourth.

No cause for concern then, when the beasts had another cold night to contend with. Nor when, next day, a snowstorm enveloped them on the top of the last pass before the Moor. Again we had opted for a cross-country route. Scorning the glen through to Altnafeadh and then the main road to Kingshouse, we struck out in a straight line over the top. It was partly a concession to the stalker at Altnafeadh who was worried that we might foul the half-mile of television cable that trailed from his house to a hill-top aerial, partly a concession to the ponies since the glen was one long peat bog, and partly to ensure that the beasts had another whole day off roads. There was also a bit of bravado behind it. The belated discovery that we got on best when not following so-called drove roads had had a wonderfully liberating effect. Inviting possibilities opened in all directions and, were it not for commitments ahead, the temptation to strike out east for Black Corries and Loch Laidon would have been irresistible.

At well over 2,000 feet the pass was the highest we would cross. Grouse rocketed from underfoot and stags scattered to left and right, wheeling to roar a protest before charging out of sight. A flock of birds that looked like fieldfares, the harbingers of winter, fluttered past heading for English stubble. The snow came in unexpected flurries. Flakes alternately whirled up from below, flew horizontally across, or floated placidly down. It was like being in one of those snowstorm paper-weights. The ground grew no whiter because the same flakes were being used again and again.

Without so much as stopping for breath we plunged over the crest, hugging the flank of Ben a Chrulaiste for shelter. For once the boys were actually pulling away from us and racing down to the Moor. Only Matilda held back. She didn't approve of impetuosity. She held her head high with horns branching like the capital of a totem pole. Framed against the snowy turmoil her outlandish profile took on a wild and prehistoric nobility. No other cow – unless it were a yak or a bison – could have looked so in her element. Had we left her there with the stags and the grouse she would have been content, worrying a bite from under the winter's snows and in spring seeking out a secluded corrie in which to have her calf.

'Come on old girl. We can do better than that.' She shook her head as if to clear it of dim ancestral promptings and slowly lowered herself down the hillside.

Flat, black and hostile the Moor of Rannoch unrolled itself below. On the A82 an occasional car raced away into the distance while black storm-clouds drifted up Glen Etive and enveloped the Buachaille. There was no other movement, no other life. 'All, every beauty, every thing vanishes before we reach the King's House,' wrote Dr MacCulloch. 'The hideous, interminable, open moor of Rannoch is spread before us, a huge and dreary Serbonian bog, a desert of blackness and vacuity and solitude and death; the death of nature.' Unable to leave it at that he tried again on the next page. This time the Moor was 'an ocean of blackness and bogs, a world before chaos, not so good as chaos since its elements are only rocks and bogs with a few pools of water, bogs of Styx and waters of Cocytus'. Every writer pulled out the stops for Rannoch but not all found it so hideous. Robert Southey, the poet laureate, who toured the Highlands with Thomas Telford in 1819, was quite enthusiastic. The mountains he had found inferior to those of his beloved Lake District but the Moor admitted of no comparison; it had 'a grand character of desolation' that was both unique and impressive.

In what must be the largest wilderness in the British Isles 'the King's House' is truly an oasis. It has the only trees for miles, the only electricity, the only shelter, the only bar. Not that it is the sort of place to which anyone pops round of an evening. Instead of 'regulars' Kingshouse relies on casualties – stranded motorists, benighted climbers, crippled skiers. Men on their last legs stagger in from the moor with sodden backpacks, empty jerry cans, frostbite and hard luck stories. When not besieged by the anorak brigade it is about as convivial as a bus shelter.

Southey thought it passable. There was no bread but the mutton was good and he was offered 'turkey's eggs' (more probably grouse's). Other travellers formed rather a different opinion. 'Not a bed fit for a decent person to sleep in nor any provisions', noted one; 'has more the appearance of a hog's stye than an Inn', wrote another. Most damning of all was Dorothy Wordsworth. 'Never did I see such a miserable wretched place . . . as dirty as a house after a sale on a rainy day.' The linen was damp, the service deplorable and the food disgusting. It was also extremely noisy, the month being September and the drovers much in evidence. Southey thought the place was probably a gold mine but according to the Wordsworths' maid it changed hands every year or two. Then, as now, it had an impersonal air. At a time when 'two monsoons' were an Englishman's life expectancy in the East, two winters on Rannoch were usually enough for the landlord of Kingshouse. Few inns were less troubled by competition and few had less incentive to please. In the eighteenth century, instead of charging a rent, the Government was actually obliged to offer a grant to keep it open.

Kingshouse also claims the distinction of being the oldest inn in Scotland; as do several other establishments. Although there probably was a hut here, dispensing the product of the local stills, from earliest times, it was only with the construction of the Military road from Stirling to Fort William that it acquired any recognised status. As distinct from the Parliamentary roads – the work of Telford, Mitchell and their assistants as Parliamentary Commissioners for Highland Roads and Bridges in the first decades of the nineteenth century – the Military roads represent an earlier phase of Highland road-building. The military crackdown which followed the Jacobite risings of 1715 and 1745 resulted in the garrisoning of Forts William, Augustus and George (the last near Inverness) and it was to maintain these garrisons that General Wade and his successors built the Military roads.

> Had you seen these roads before they were made
> You would hold up your hands and bless Marshall Wade.

They were in fact the first roads designed for wheeled traffic that were ever built in the Highlands; but, in spite of the well-known couplet, it is doubtful whether when the local population held up their hands, it was to bless the Marshall. 'I am not sure that they [the Highlanders] will always forsake their old short cuts for the pleasure of going ten miles round on hard gravel,' wrote a contemporary. Lieutenant Burt of the Fort George garrison agreed; the new roads were quite unsuitable for cattle or for Highland ponies, both being unshod. Unlike Telford's roads, Wade's were never designed to stimulate the Highland economy nor to take account of civilian needs.

Yet paradoxically, though few and soon in poor repair, they probably did more for the cattle trade than the far more extensive Parliamentary network. To thrive, what the cattle trade needed was not surfaced roads but settled conditions; and law and order were only enforceable when there were roads. In the early eighteenth century the most lawless areas were not in the remote fastnesses of the north and north-west but in Lochaber, where MacDonnell of Barrisdale and the Camerons were the miscreants, and in the skirts of the High-

lands between Loch Lomond and Glen Lyon, the hunting
ground of the MacGregors (including Rob Roy) and of the
'Breadalbane Men'. These areas were precisely those which
the Military roads most affected. In the 1720s and 1730s Wade
built a road along the length of the Great Glen, thus giving
access to Lochaber, and another from Crieff past Loch Tay to
Tummel Bridge. This latter went on to Inverness and Fort
Augustus by way of the Drumochter and Corrieyairack passes;
it is the best known of Wade's roads but it kept well to the east
of Rannoch Moor. It was not until 1752 and the construction
of the road from Stirling to Fort William by way of Kingshouse that the Moor, the raiders' principal retreat, was pene-
trated.

> They [cattle raiders] go out in parties of ten to thirty men, traverse
> large tracts of mountains till they arrive at the Low Lands, where
> they design to commit their depredations which they choose to do
> in places distant from the glens which they inhabit. They drive the
> stolen cattle in the night time and in the day remain in the tops of
> the mountains or in the woods . . .

Wade rightly emphasised that the raiders preferred to operate
at a distance and to move rapidly back into safe ground. For
the Breadalbane Men, the MacGregors and perhaps even the
Camerons the safest ground was the Moor of Rannoch.
According to the Old Statistical Account, before 1745 the
robbers of Rannoch 'laid the whole country, from Stirling to
Coupar of Angus, under contribution, obliging the inhabitants
to pay them Black Meal [blackmail], as it is called, to save
their property from being plundered'.

> This [the Moor] was the centre of this kind of traffic. In the
> months of September and October they gathered to the number of
> about 300, built temporary huts, drank whisky all the time,
> settled accounts for stolen cattle, and received balances. It would
> have required a regiment to have brought a thief from that
> country.

The Black Watch, formed in 1740 from companies of loyal
Highlanders raised by Wade, was just such a regiment but the

raiding seems to have continued even after the suppression of the 1745 rising. Eventually it was thanks to the road that it never revived.

Round Rannoch Moor the droves did actually follow the road. It offered soft going on the sides, bridges over the burns, and a firm footing across the bogs. To wander off it would have been to invite disaster. If they managed to find a path through the worst peat hags in Scotland there was still, even after 1752, the risk of being waylaid.

In 1981 the matter looked rather different. Even the road was not safe. News that a drove of cattle was heading through the Highlands inevitably stirred old memories and reports were constantly coming in of raiding parties which might or might not be about to make off with our beasts. 'Beware Glen Garry,' whispered a complete stranger at Glenelg; 'We Mac-Gregors have our reputation to look to,' boasted a young blood. Assuming that twentieth-century raiders would travel by road, perhaps even use a lorry, there seemed little danger of skull-duggery in the remote glens behind Ben Nevis. But on Rannoch – especially at Kingshouse – we were a sitting target.

Permission for the night's stance – even on Rannoch Moor one needs permission to park a herd of cattle – applied to 'the vicinity of Blackrock Cottage'. Like the hotel, the cottage lies some two hundred yards back from the main Glasgow–Fort William road but on the opposite side. Low and snug with its black roof barely peaking above the heather, it belongs to the Scottish Ladies Mountaineering Federation and it was strictly out of bounds to drovers. (We had pleaded but the ladies had been adamant.) As for its vicinity this was unfenced and indistinguishable from the rest of the Moor. It mattered little, therefore, where we pitched the tents or how the electric fence was strung out. All was equally exposed. On three sides the moor stretched away in gloomy uniformity, just too broken to afford a glimpse of the lochans which puddle its surface when seen from above and just too level to offer any kind of shelter. Only to the south did the ground quickly rise but here lay the White Corries ski-lift with a good access road that came even closer than the main road.

It was also common knowledge that raiders were in readiness. 'The Ballachulish Boys', whoever they might be, were said to have been perfecting their plans for weeks and since we were to be at Black Mount for a ceilidh the following evening, they must have deduced that tonight we would be somewhere near Kingshouse. At dusk a small car parked itself nearby. The young lady at the wheel claimed that she was 'The West Highland Way Ranger'. On balance this seemed improbable; the title was too bizarre and the incumbent too glamorous. She drove off west down Glen Coe towards Ballachulish. We were not taken in.

It was too late to change the disposition of the stance. The tents were between the beasts and the road which would at least give the raiders a trek through the heather. It was also turning into the foulest of nights. A raw gale charged across the Moor chucking rain, sleet and hail ahead of it. We were ten for dinner, friends (or reinforcements) having come up from Appin and Loch Fyneside bearing gifts and good cheer. But the noise of the gale killed all conversation. We sat round the tent on bales of hay feeling absurdly formal and awkward. The pressure lamps contrived to make the salami look green and the claret phosphorescent; thanks to Russell's ginger wine the whisky *was* green. Later we adjourned to the comfort of the hotel and then, having checked the beasts, crawled into ever-damp sleeping bags.

The night continued wild. It was inconceivable that anyone would venture forth in such conditions purely for a prank. If the beasts were still there, fine; if they were not, there was nothing to be done about it till the morning. No point then in getting up. Banish the thought. Besides, the torch was missing.

Dawn was a long time coming. Eventually I lost patience,

got up, and found that, in so far as it was going to, day had already broken. Grey watery cloud sponged its way across the heather; between the two you could see only a few sodden yards. The beasts were out of sight; either they were sitting down in the heather or they were up at the far end of the enclosure. But ah, no, the red and yellow wires were slack, trailing dismally between the poles. The fence must be down. Without investigating further I sounded the alarm.

According to both Burt and Pennant, Highland herdsmen were excellent trackers. They might follow the trail of stolen cattle for days and, knowing the hoofprints of their own, could even track them through other herds. Additionally, 'the heath or heather, being pressed by the foot, retains the impression, or at least some remains of it, for a long while before it rises again.' Not having learnt the hoof marks of our beasts we would have to follow what Burt delicately described as 'the other visible marks left behind by the cattle'. In fact he was quite right about the heather. The wake of the herd through its deep swell was plainly visible. It led not onto the road but back and up into the lee of Meall a Bhuiridh, 'the hill of roaring'. We had gone only a few hundred yards when we heard from in front not a roar but a deep and familiar lowing. Ickle Brindle, his horns not much more than the knobs of a roe buck, stuck his teddy-bear-like head up out of the heather. There were three of his smaller brethren nearby.

'Boys, boys, boys. Boys, boys, boys.' Gavin gave his usual breakfast call and was greeted by a chorus of mooing from up in the cloud. Careering down the hill with bits of heather still sticking out of their mouths they nearly knocked us over. It was a joyful reunion. With protestations of abject loyalty the boys grovelled apologetically while the drovers pledged never again to pen them in such an exposed spot. Great was the fuss made by both parties. In a happy gaggle all returned to camp for the heartiest of breakfasts. Ahead lay an easy walk along and beside Wade's road to Black Mount. There tomorrow would be a rest day while the drovers recovered from their

ceilidh. Then there were just the final fifty miles to Crieff. A
week should do it.

If Kingshouse has an unhappy reputation, its counterpart, the
inn of Inveroran at the southern end of the Military road
across the Moor, was and is much more appealing. Flanked by
ancient Scots pines, a remnant of the Great Caledonian Forest
which once blanketed even the Moor with its kindly cover, it
stands on the shore of Loch Tulla. On September 4th 1803
Dorothy and William Wordsworth noted the trunks of dead
trees, partly cut down to flush out the cattle thieves, sticking
out of the peat as they came over the Moor from Kingshouse.

> The road, . . . after having made a curve above the tarn [Loch
> Tulla] was seen winding through the trees on the other side
> [Inveroran] and luckily for us, a drove of cattle happened to be
> passing there at the very time, a stream coursing the road with
> off-stragglers to the borders of the lake and under the trees on the
> sloping-ground.

At Inveroran, 'a thatched house without a sign', they had an
indifferent breakfast. It failed to dampen their spirits. Thanks
mainly to the cattle the Wordsworths were 'in a bustle of
enjoyment'. For droves 'stamped a character upon places else
unremembered – not an individual character but the soul, the
spirit, and solitary simplicity of many a Highland region.'
They were also deliciously picturesque; Dorothy was itching
to get out her sketchpad. Even the scene in the Inveroran
kitchen was 'rememberable'. Drovers with their dogs sat in a
circle round the peat fire each with 'a mess of porridge in a
wooden bowl on his knee'. Women and children were bustling
round the fringes and the smokey air, 'the natural indoor
atmosphere of Scotland', gave the whole gathering a pleasing
harmony. 'I would willingly have given £20 to have been able
to take a lively picture of it.'

Half a century later the stance beside the inn at Inveroran
became a matter of national debate. Lord Breadalbane, the

laird of Black Mount estate (and of a good many others) attempted to move the stance to a new site in Tyndrum six miles away. The proposal was resisted by the drovers on the grounds that this would make the distance from Kingshouse too great for their beasts to cover in a single day. 'MacGregor and others', representing drovers from as far afield as Wester Ross, Skye and the Outer Hebrides, took their case to court. In the Court of Session their contention that a right of stance was essential to a right of way was upheld. But in 1848 Breadalbane appealed to his peers in the House of Lords. Although his case was based not on the need 'to make way for cultivation or improvement of any kind but', in the words of the *London Daily News*, 'to foster the barbarous and puerile passion for artificial wild sports' the Lords quashed the previous decision and accepted Breadalbane's claim that stance rights, however ancient and necessary, had no basis in law because they would infringe on the rights of the proprietor.

In practice a compromise was reached and a stance was arranged at Bridge of Orchy, two miles beyond Inveroran. But the principle had been rejected and although rights of way were not in this instance in question, it seriously undermined the whole trade. Droving was thus under threat several decades before the coming of the railways provided an alternative. Significantly the issue hinged on a legal interpretation of landownership which was foreign to the Highlands in that traditionally land had belonged to the whole clan, not its chief. And no less significantly, it was in the interests of sport, not agriculture, that droving rights were challenged. (Sheep were already as important as cattle with seventy thousand of the former passing through Inveroran each year but just eight to ten thousand of the latter.) Individually none of these factors brought droving to a standstill. It survived the coming of sheep, it survived the new concept of landownership, and it survived the formation of sporting estates. But in the course of the nineteenth century each of these innovations tended gradually to regulate, contain and hence diminish a trade which was essentially and originally uninhibited and free-ranging. In the Highlands 'drove roads', 'official stances' and the like may be seen as a contradiction in terms.

In so far as we increasingly preferred to ignore such things we were, I believe, closer to the spirit and traditions of the trade. There was therefore no contradiction in foregoing both the Inveroran and Bridge of Orchy stances in favour of installing the boys in a spacious and well-fenced park at Black Mount itself. This fringe of Rannoch Moor is just in Argyll; we were on home ground. Captain Ben Coutts, the factor of Black Mount estate, had been one of the few pundits of Scottish farming who had consistently offered assistance and encouragement. And the MC for the evening's ceilidh was to be Bobby Andrews, the Dalmally–Bridge of Orchy postman who for ten years had been splashing up the track to our house to exchange commiserations about the fishing and the weather and, while he was about it, to deliver the letters.

There was also Hamish Menzies, the Arnold Palmer of Argyllshire curling. He sat me down to eggs and spam fritters as the rain crashed down outside and in this compromising situation I was discovered by a procession of cattle, ponies and drovers who trooped past the window; they had covered the eight miles from Kingshouse in a record five hours.

In any other place, in any other company, an artificial ceilidh would have been a disaster. But at Black Mount neither commercial sponsorship nor the reappearance of television cameras managed to inhibit the kindness, decorum and good cheer of true Highland hospitality.

This 'rememberable' interlude on the shores of Loch Tulla was finally notable for the appearance of a very young, very old gentleman, Mr Alec MacDougall of Clachan. He arrived as the cattle were being put through the footbath, but far from deriding the operation he was genuinely impressed with the condition of the beasts; he was even complimentary about the standard of herdsmanship. It was a valued commendation. Alec MacDougall is the son of 'the last of the true Argyllshire drovers', Dugald MacDougall – 'even suppose one would think it a simple thing, there was an art in doing it properly too, to give man and beast a chance, yes.'

12

'Sad the shieling'

BLACK MOUNT TO GLEN LYON

'What say you to Blondie there, eh? Aaaaah, look at the saddle now. You fancy a bit of pope's eye don't you John? If we was to have a word with the auctioneer. . . . Well, y'know, the price'd be fair. Aye, I'm telling you.' George, back from his sabbatical, was seeing the boys with a certain detachment. 'I'll find his keep – och, he'll come on great – and we'll put him away to the slaughterers next autumn. Ye'll have room in yer freezer then? Half and half, yes?'

Though by no means sentimental about animals, Julia was horrified. Butchering our own boys?

'George, how could you? You'll be wanting to chop up Matilda next.' It was unthinkable. Julia was not even resigned to the inevitable – that barring Matilda all were destined for the pot. 'Can't we find some safari park or some stately home that'll buy them? As an attraction. I mean they are a bit famous. They deserve a reprieve. They've earned it.'

That would be the ideal solution. Russell, the hotelier and always the voice of cool common sense, dismissed it. The most the boys had earned was a good price in the ring and an honourable mention on the menu. There was a rumour that some buyer planned to prolong their celebrity by serving them up at a farewell dinner for Scotland's World Cup squad. Now that was more like it. We could be sure that their last months would be spent amongst ease and plenty and they would end their days in the noblest of causes. Mentally he was already garnishing them with parsley butter and watercress; thick and rare with a few spears of broccoli they would be more than a match for Argentine corned beef.

The rest of us were nauseated. JP, though willing to assist personally in the slaughter of the yellow bronco that had it in for his shins, canvassed a continuation of the drove down to the traditional fattening grounds in East Anglia and the English Midlands; with cattle so accustomed to droving it should not, he opined, be difficult to find a team of drovers. Chris, for one, was game. The boys were proving to be the veterinary surgeon's dream patients, demanding constant attention and expensive drugs yet remaining in excellent health and therefore a fine testimonial to his skills.

Gavin took no part in the discussion. It was beneath the attention of the romantic adventurer. Besides, he was off to Africa in a fortnight. Ivory poaching, now there was something worth getting worked up about. But slaughtering a few bullocks? Irrelevant. I rather agreed, not with the reasoning but with the conclusion. If prices were bad, if we lost any beasts, instead of living on steak or safari-ing in Africa we would be years just paying off the deficit. No drove was a success or a failure until the last beast had been knocked down to the last buyer. Speculation was premature. We still had a way to go, some of it anything but easy, and if the beasts got wind of this discussion we would have to manage it without their co-operation.

Although within earshot, the boys were preoccupied with their evening feed. Apart from Goldie, one of those who had suffered with transit fever on Skye, who now again had a temperature, all twenty-six were looking good. The floppy horns syndrome had apparently been stopped by the change in diet. The flakiness was peeling away like coarse dandruff; underneath there was glossy new horn tapering to points that looked as if they were fresh from the pencil sharpener. Two of the beasts that had been rested because of sore feet were fit enough to rejoin, there had been no further cases of lameness, and ahead lay two days of cross-country.

It was October 29th and we were installed in a bothy called Gorton, eight miles east of Black Mount. According to most authorities the route was again 'wrong'; the main drove route from Kingshouse to Inveroran continued south to cross the watershed at Tyndrum and thence on through Crianlarich and Glen Dochart to Killin. But this was also the line of the main road and today, for much of the way, it would have been impossible to avoid it. Besides, there was a much more intriguing alternative. Angus MacGillivray, Oban's best judge of Highland cattle and a great nephew of Donald, the Mull drover, was pretty sure that he remembered his father saying that in Donald's day the drovers preferred to go from Bridge of Orchy over to Glen Lyon. It may have been to avoid the road, it may have been to avoid the tolls and the stance charges; drovers were very canny. Whatever the reason, they went, he thought, by way of Auch glen at the back of Ben Dorain and then down to Loch Lyon.

'There was a village there in those days, six houses at least, and good grazing. But, you see, the level of the water was raised when they built the hydro dam. The village, it must be under the water now; and so is the drovers' track.'

Julia had investigated this route and declared it too dangerous; as with Loch Quoich, raising the water had flooded all the level low ground and the lower slopes leaving a shoreline of steep rock interspersed with boggy hollows.

But yet a further possibility emerged in conversation with the keeper at the head of Glen Lyon. Bob Bisset is rather more than a keeper. Mention Glen Lyon and someone will refer you to Bisset. A gruff and stocky figure in plain tweed kilt and home-made brogues, he roams the hills muttering snippets of Robbie Burns and seeing off the riff-raff of the present age. To Bob every convenience of the twentieth century is a red rag. Frozen peas, artificial fibres, television, waterproofs, insulation, fertilisers, development agencies, chipboard, poly-anything – all are anathema. As you enter the Bissets' sanctum, a trim little cottage crouched defiantly beneath the hydro dam and with a plume of peat smoke peeling from its chimney, you pause to make a mental body search. It is not a concession to Bob's values and certainly not a fear of incurring his wrath; he is, on acquaintance, the kindest and most tolerant anachronism. It is more a question of acknowledging the perfect decorum of his lifestyle and dreading lest one should defile it. Removing a digital watch or a nylon anorak is as natural as shedding shoes and leather belt on the threshold of a Hindu temple.

Inside, twenty-one clocks, many of them grandfathers, tick away the decades. From the remaining wall-space diverse heads and horns, ancient fowling pieces, framed pictures of Burns, and stuffed pine martens crowd in towards the brass fender and the glowing range. Above it, the *pièce de résistance* is an enormous clock face with a miniature of Burns inset at six o'clock. Below, on the rug, an ancient and battle-scarred terrier sleeps on while Mrs B. makes the tea and Bob rummages amongst a pile of half-made brogues for the whisky.

'Invermeran, that's the way you've to come. Tyndrum? Auch? Goodness no. Why do you think there was an inn at Invermeran? It was the stance. That was the way they came into the glen. Did you no hear of the lassie there? She was the last, the last to stay there. They said she was, you know, simple, not-quite-right-in-the-head. She would run to the door every evening and just stand there, aye, like this, hand to her ear, listening. Aye, just listening.'

'For what, Bob?'

'For what? For what? For Heaven's sake. Why, for the cattle of course. She was waiting, listening, for the cattle. That was the way they came I tell you.'

On the map Invermeran does not exist. Uncertain how the Ordnance Survey stood in Bob's estimation I deemed it politic not to produce the relevant sheet. But obviously, since 'inver' means mouth, it must be, or have been, at the mouth of Glen Meran. And on close scrutiny it did indeed appear that the lowest breach in the ring of mountains that walls in the head of

Glen Lyon – and therefore the likely drove route – was between Gorton and Glen Meran.

This gap in the mountains must also be the 'very remarkable Pass to and from the Isle of Skye' referred to in military reports of 1749 and 1750 and sometimes called Carn. From extracts quoted by Professor Haldane it lay half-way between Achallader and Loch Lyon and was not only an important drove route but also the bolt hole by which cattle thieves smuggled their booty from the Lowlands on to the Moor. In 1749, only three years before the Military road was built, an ambush was laid here to catch just such a gang. Sixty years later Telford proposed that his main road to Skye should also use this pass. The proposal failed because, significantly, 'the personal convenience of the proprietors is not immediately concerned' – a candid admission that in the final analysis roads materialised to serve the interests not of the drovers but of the landowners.

To judge from old maps, Loch Lyon more than trebled its surface area when the hydro dam was built. Glen Meran, instead of ending near the head of the loch as now, then joined the river Lyon at the mouth of the loch. Invermeran and its inn, like the village mentioned by MacGillivray and several other settlements, are now a hundred feet under water. The only way to get from Glen Meran round to the dam involves edging along four miles of steep and broken hillside. Bob said there was a track of sorts but 'you'll need to take your time'.

More immediately there was an obstacle on the Gorton side of the pass. In front of the bothy runs a sizeable burn and beyond it, on a raised embankment, British Rail's West Highland Line. At eight p.m. the Fort William to Euston sleeper came rattling across the Moor and trundled past above us; an attendant was turning down crisp cotton sheets. On the map the line is interrupted by numerous 'sheep creeps', low passages by which sheep can cross under the track. 'Cattle creeps' are less common. The local shepherd gave it as his opinion that the cattle would probably fit through the Gorton creep but definitely not the ponies. They would need to head for the gated crossing four miles up the line and then return on the other side.

Unfortunately the ponies had a full day in prospect without this extra detour. Since it was impossible to get a vehicle within four miles of the next stance in Glen Meran they were going to be fully laden with feedstuffs for a day's march that was again dangerously soft. For once they were the focus of all attention. In deference to their predicament only two drovers, plus the dogs, would stay with the cattle. The rest of the party, themselves also carrying packs, would assist Julia with the ponies.

At first light the beasts were fed, the drovers breakfasted and the ponies loaded. We left Gorton with reluctance. The bothy with its pine pannelling and its little sash windows still glazed was the best we had encountered. Beside it grassy sheep-pens had comfortably accommodated the cattle and not far away there was ample firewood in the stumps of long-dead Scots pines. This was the southern edge of Rannoch Moor but already birches high on the slopes of Ben a Chreachain to the south presaged gayer surroundings and grassier going.

By nine a.m. we were across the burn that runs in front of the bothy and working the cattle into the creep. Provided they kept their heads down – and provided a train did not take them by surprise – it was fairly straightforward. What the creep lacked in headroom it made up for in width; hence the beasts had only to lower their horns, not twist them. We regrouped beside a clump of rowans just above the track. With a long steepish pull over the shoulder of Ben a Chreachain offering the shortest route across the watershed and into Glen Meran, Gavin and the dogs went on ahead with the cattle. The rest of us, somehow, would get the ponies through.

While two people hacked away at the stony floor of the passage to increase its height, Mhari, usually the most amenable of the ponies who also happened to be the smallest, was unloaded and primed for action. Then Russell and Julia hauled from in front and the rest of us shoved from behind. She entered the passage with a couple of inches to spare and, where the ground rose at the top end, just scraped through. Ponies do not crawl; but with one now through, the others showed a willingness to limbo that suggested an exciting alternative to show-jumping. Skewing, rolling, and slithering, Eilidh and then Rona wheedled their way beneath the concrete roof. Meanwhile the shepherd stood aside fiddling with his camera. He was still insisting that we would need to go round by the crossing as we reloaded and set off up the hill.

High on the slopes of Ben a Chreachain a halt was called to readjust the loads. (To keep them dry the cattle cobs had been put in polythene sacks but, however ingeniously lashed, these had a habit of slipping down the pack saddles.) Below us to the left the floor of the glen was another of those peat-choked watersheds. However inviting they looked on the map it was not along but beside and above such passes that cattle were driven. At some point soon we would have to cut down into the glen and get onto its eastern side, but until past the worst of the peat we would stick to the hill. Compared to the stark Grey Corries above Lairig Leacach these hills were paradise. Snipe whirred from underfoot and in the hollows crooked birches stood in a pool of their own leaves.

We were now as high as we needed to go. In fact we were touching the ceiling of cloud so that, looking back over the Moor, one got a fly's-eye view of the world. The cloud receded into a flat and grey horizon; but in places it must have been broken, for shafts of sunlight stabbed down towards the heaving carpet of heather below. One streaked across a desolate tarn, another glinted on the distant whitewash and roughcast of Rannoch station. Then the silvery-grey pall of a shower intervened and we hurried on, backs and packs to the sleet and the Moor, heading south and down.

The hillsides of Glen Meran and Glen Lyon are truly another world. Instead of the black acidic peat and the scratchy heather, here are grassy downs of a dazzling green.

13 Eilidh with Julia, Rona with Russell, Mhairi with panniers

14 Cowering from gale no. 13 in an airy shed at Invermeran, Loch Lyon. Before the water level in the loch was raised there was here a drovers' inn and a thriving township

The burns slide sleekly over gravel beds, their banks dotted with more rowans and silver birches. Just across the watershed and already the rainfall is lower and the ground quicker to drain. This is some of the richest hill grazing where once every corrie and fold had its name and its patrons. For these were prime shielings, those vital summer pastures which made the Highlands such ideal cattle country.

*   *   *

To understand the importance of cattle in the history of the Highlands one must look beyond purely social and economic factors. The image of that lonely and deranged waif listening each night for the cattle to come through the pass to Invermeran expresses a simple and still widely accepted equation: cattle equalled the good times. They were not just 'the wealth of the Highlands' – the same would be said of sheep – but they were peculiarly the wealth of the Highland people. They epitomised the old social order before the egalitarian clan system collapsed and the cash economy took over. They were associated with an era of vitality, independence and near-sufficiency which, as destitution, depopulation and social injustice set in, came to be regarded as a golden age. Just as all that was bad – eviction, emigration, oppression – is blamed on the sheep, so all that was good – self-respect, industry and artistic expression – is linked with the idea of cattle.

To put dates and events to this notion is extremely difficult. Conditions throughout the Highlands, even definitions of the Highlands, varied enormously. Cattle prices and trading conditions fluctuated and there were many incidental factors; the introduction of the potato, for instance, or the kelp bonanza, had dramatic and distorting short-term and local effects. Nonetheless the generalisation may stand. Cattle farming methods favoured the principle of most land being held in common and so underpinned the clan system. They were also labour-intensive and hence, compared to sheep farming, en-couraged a comparatively dense level of population. During the summer the cattle's treading and manuring enriched the hill pastures and during the winter their dung was used to fertilise the arable ground on which the people depended for their corn. Cattle were also used to pull the plough in some areas. It was a system of mixed farming which included a few goats, sheep and hens as well as arable but one in which the predominant and regenerative role was played by cattle.

The same is true of many Third World countries today and nowhere more so than India where the importance of cattle remains enshrined in religious tradition. In the Highlands the cow never became sacred but here too, by all but the lairds, it was rarely killed for meat. It was the milk, cream, curds, butter and cheese which the Highlander cherished. And as the provider of these necessities cows, in the Highlands as in India, came to be regarded as symbolic of all that was munificent, fertile and generous. Milk yields were highest in the summer when the cattle were pastured on the rich hill grazings and thus the months when people and cattle moved up to the shielings were a time of plenty and excitement.

> There, bounding together
> On the grass and the heather
> And free from the tether
>   The heifers shall throng . . .
>
> And there shall my Mary
> With her faithful one tarry,
> And never be weary
>   In the hollows to stray.

William Ross, born at Broadford in 1762, used the image of the free and easy life of the shielings to celebrate the youthful release of love and beauty. Many other Gaelic poets pursued the same theme. 'Where a cow is, a woman will be; where a woman is, temptation will be,' warned St Columba, the Irish apostle to the Picts and Scots. It was peculiarly the job of the women and children to take care of the cattle. They herded them on the hillside, milked them in the fold, and handled all the cheese and butter-making. At this time of the year the men would be busy cutting peat, thatching, cutting kelp or fishing. A snatched visit to the shielings was thus imbued with heavy sexual connotations. Rocks, hollows and thickets became places of assignation and, if it is valid to judge from the Gaelic-English translations, cattle acquired a sexual symbolism while the topography of the shielings was exploited for erotic associations.

Rob Donn, the Sutherland poet (born 1714), worked as a drover in his youth and while busy with the cattle at the Crieff tryst composed a love-song to his sweetheart at home which combines strict propriety of sentiment with distinctly erotic suggestion.

> Easy is my bed, it is easy,
> But it is not to sleep that I incline;
> The wind whistles northwards, northwards,
> And my thoughts move with it.
> More pleasant were it to be with thee
> In the little glen of the calves,
> Than to be counting of droves
> In the enclosures of Crieff.
>
> Great is my esteem for the maiden
> Toward whose dwelling the north wind blows.
> She is ever cheerful, sportive, kindly,
> Without folly, without vanity, without pride.
> True is her heart – were I under hiding,
> And fifty men in pursuit of my footsteps,
> I should find protection when they surround me most closely
> In the sweet recess of that shieling.
>
> Oh for the day of my turning my face homeward,
> That I may see the maiden of beauty:-
> Joyful will it be for me to be with thee,
> Fair girl with the long heavy locks.
> Choice of all places for deer hunting
> Are the brindled rock and the ridge!
> How sweet at evening to be dragging the slain deer
> Downwards along the piper's cairn . . .

As is the way, by the time he returned to Sutherland the maid in question had been successfuly wooed by another. In one of his most famous verses Rob Donn bemoaned her loss by again evoking the shieling.

> O sad is the shieling
> And gone are its joys!
> All harsh and unfeeling
> To me now its noise.
> Sweet Anna who warbled
> As sweet as the merle
> Forsook me, my honey-mouthed
> Merry-lipped girl.

The hills between Glen Lyon and Glen Orchy were immortalised by the greatest of all Gaelic nature poets, Duncan Ban MacIntyre (born 1724). Addicted to the chase he had explored every corrie and glen and used the imagery of hind, doe and fawn in preference to that of cow, heifer and calf. Nevertheless, 'I earned my living for a time/at shielings that I knew full well,/with frolic, fun, flirtation,/enjoying maiden's tender fellowship.' And his *Summer Song* included a detailed description of life at the shielings.

> Every herd, assembled on the upper heights –
> 'tis to the shieling they will all proceed:
> come milk and cattle-pairing without stint,
> and mounting crest on the maid's milking pail;
> for heifers, youngest and most vigorous,
> that fetter time have not experienced –
> for these the brown-tressed damsel hath a song,
> soothing them gently with her simple lays.

> Truly attractive are the young calves
> in the precincts of that fold at eventime;
> they are white-bellied, dappled and stout-legged;
> white-flanked, white-backed, white-nosed with shoulders high;
> also brown-hued, jet black, going two by two,
> yellow, grey-white, blood-red, remarkable;
> lithe, smooth of hide, erect, of comely form;
> full soft and sleek the surface of their hide.

Duncan Ban's sweetheart and inspiration, though a girl of means who would bring her own dowry of cows and calves, also went to the shielings; as she milked the cattle her skin was 'as white as the rocks of quartz', her complexion 'as soft as the bog cotton', and her breasts 'as steep and pointed as the loftiest peaks'.

Liberated from the smoky hearth, the domestic routine and the stern surveillance of elders, young girls blossomed at the shielings and were then at their most available. The shielings, and the cattle that made them necessary, thus epitomised not only summer and the season of plenty but also youth, frivolity, flirtation and song. Hence the complex and rich sediment of psychological associations which, along with the social and economic, still cling to the memory of cattle and dairy farming in the Highlands.

★   ★   ★

At Invermeran, instead of an inn, a village, or a choice of shielings, the only shelter on offer today is a vast and draughty prefabricated shed. On the concrete floor we laid out sleeping bags and watched the dung-rich water from a flooded sheep dip advancing towards them. Because we were out of reach of the Land Rover, tents were not available and food and drink were in limited supply. It was not an evening for frivolity let alone flirtation and song. The fourteenth gale of the month tore at the loose sheets of corrugated iron occasionally wrenching one loose and sending it crashing down the roof and out into the night. To add to the discomfort, while smashing firewood, I impaled the heel of my boot, the heels of three pairs of socks, and the heel of my foot on a 4-inch nail. Chris prised this cheesy kebab apart and, being for once without his formalin, doused the foot in the last few drams of Famous Grouse.

Under the circumstances it was not even a night for entertaining romantic notions above droving. Although in itself the cattle trade was full of stirring associations, could it really be said to have supported the pastoral serenity of the traditional Highland economy? In old age Duncan Ban MacIntyre, grey, toothless and unsteady, revisited Ben Dorain, the highest of the peaks between Glen Lyon and Glen Orchy. Surveying the deserted slopes, the ravaged woodlands and the abandoned shielings he blamed everything on the new craze for sheep farming. Cattle, wildlife and people had all been cleared to make way for the flocks. The villages were now empty, the fields deserted. Only the foxes survived and, since they preyed on the sheep, he wished them well.

Such sentiments made powerful poetry but questionable history. To equate the plight of the Highlands with the coming of sheep seems to overlook the little matter of chronology. The demand for wool and the discovery that Cheviot and Blackface sheep would thrive on Highland pastures did not supercede the demand for cattle but paralleled it. Both were triggered by the same exterior factors – the growth of large industrial cities and of their processing industries and the need to clothe and provision troops involved in the succession of French wars. Large-scale sheep farming was first introduced in the 1760s and by the time the cattle trade was at its climax between 1830 and 1850 the Clearances were a thing of the past in most areas. Most of the north and west was already made over to sheep runs and it was from the periphery – especially the north-east (MacCombie's country) and the Islands – that the demand for cattle was being met.

Perhaps what destroyed the fabric of Highland life, apart from military defeat and political reprisals, was not sheep or any other specific cash crop but cash crops in general. As soon as it was accepted that the Highlands were part of the wider national economy and that land should render a return in cash rather than in legions of arms-bearing clansmen, agricultural adjustments were inevitable. In Skye as early as the 1770s Dr Johnson observed that rents were being paid in the promissory notes issued by drovers. Currency was still in short supply but the credit system introduced by the droving fraternity probably did more than anything else to fuel the change-over to a cash economy and to facilitate a landlord–tenant relationship based on rents rather than loyalty. The expansion of the cattle trade and the dramatic increase in droving activity during the late eighteenth and early nineteenth centuries could therefore be seen not as the last glimmer of a golden age but as the first flash of lightning from the imminent storm. There was a 'craze' for cattle as there was for sheep and together they perhaps belong at the top of that list of much vaunted panaceas – kelp and herrings, sport and forestry, oil and tourism – which have conspicuously failed (or are failing) to reverse the depopulation and decline of the region.

But if the drovers were contributing to change, this is not to say that they were unpopular. On the contrary, whether native-born or not, they were seen as performing a vital role and, so long as they did not default, they were welcomed back year after year. In distant glens and islands they represented not only the Highlander's bank but also his newspaper. It was from the drover's busy tongue that people learned what was afoot in Crieff, Falkirk, Edinburgh, London, Waterloo. The irony of the Highland situation was that a people who were hostage to progress were also intrigued by it. The one missing element in the tragedy of the Highlands is the expected con-servatism of the people. Traveller after traveller remarked on the contrast between their economic plight and their informed and intelligent conversation. A reverence for education, the possession of a rich literary tradition and the clan system's lack of rigid class barriers all tended to make the Highlander not just one of Nature's gentlemen but also one of her scholars. Few people, once they had said their sad farewells to the homestead, were more successful in making their mark in the outside world.

'My son, now, he was a very bright lad, quick and bright. "I'll make a drover of you," thought I, "yes, a drover." ' According to Ian MacGillivray, Donald the Mull drover was shrewd, glib, even well-read. But it was this remark of another great-uncle – Donald was a bachelor 'of course' – which had lodged in Ian's memory; he repeated it several times and it seemed to speak volumes for the wit and standing of a

Highland drover. It was the quick, the bright and the curious
who were recruited as drover's lads. Corriechoillie, the dealer,
Rob Donn, the poet, and Donald the Drover had all begun
their very different careers in this way. Although there are
records of a few droving families, for the most part it seems
that the profession was open to anyone keen and clever enough
to be taken on. Like winning a scholarship it was an acknowledgement of early promise and future prospects. It also guaranteed respect. The drovers were the ones who had come to
terms with change and progress. They were welcomed not just
as bearers of news and cash but as men of insight whose knowledge of the economy and the market place could be tapped for
advice on when to sell and what to buy. In an informal way
they performed some of the services now offered by the Department of Agriculture.

As apprentices the young lads of ten and twelve handled
most of the day-to-day grind of droving. It was they who
actually kept the cattle moving by darting from one flank of
the drove to the other; it was they who leapt and shouted to
encourage them over obstacles; and they who set off in pursuit
whenever a beast strayed. By night they acted as the watch and
by day they plodded slowly, patiently, endlessly beside the
cattle.

In short they did exactly what seven adults old enough to be
their parents were now doing along the steep slopes above
Loch Lyon. Leaving the shed at Invermeran with none of the
regrets experienced at Gorton, the drove had set off with the
blustery remnants of the gale pushing us along. On the loch,
here about fifty yards wide, the waves chased beside and
below us while the clouds raced past above. Showers of hail
and patches of sun joined in the mad stampede as they flitted
along the grassy hills on the opposite shore.

But if the day cried out for a canter on the ponies and a
cracking pace from the cattle, the terrain did not. To guide the
drove in, Bob Bisset had walked out to join us. This was
always a mark of true hospitality but here it was also some-

thing of a necessity, the track being little more than a scratch across the hillside. In places it wriggled down a trickle of stones, or crossed a chasm on a couple of slippery planks; rarely was it more than a few feet from the rocky drop into the loch. In deference to the danger George put a rope on Matilda and, for the first time since Skye, led her in front, their combined experience being guaranteed to find the safest going and to keep the pace to a sedate and cautious crawl.

After five painful hours the track zig-zagged down to the dam, the roadhead, and Bob's cottage. We were safely across the watershed, into Perthshire, and back in civilisation. A dram was in order; but Mrs Bisset's three-course lunch for seven surpassed any definition of courtesy.

That afternoon I drove into Aberfeldy in search of an anti-tetanus injection. Glen Lyon in the autumn is one of the great Highland attractions. Long, level and stately, it glories in a woodland canopy so dense and varied that it seems not Highland at all. Beech, birch, oak and pine combine with more exotic stands of lime, poplar, sycamore and larch to produce a riot of sylvan colour. Rust and russet, copper and bronze, amber and gold shimmered in the afternoon sun. The poplar's plume of oriole yellow was as unreal as the crossbill crimson of the feathery rowan. Only the sober alder and the crow-black pine recalled a sterner reality. Deep drifts of leaves blocked the road and, as the car ploughed through, it left a whirling swarm in its wake.

On the way back the breeze was teasing an autumn blizzard from the birches. Beyond Meggernie Castle the glen opened out until, on a now treeless roadside near Kenknock, the drove at last hove into view. They were padding along beside the tarmac with a single small boy in charge. He must have been about ten years old, the son perhaps of a local stalker. Someone had lent him a stick and though he had to clamber onto a dyke to see over the backs of the beasts, he was moving them along as steadily and patiently as the most experienced stockman. The drovers were holding back to watch him at work. It was hard to believe that he had not walked cattle before.

Next day, a Sunday, Alexander, our eight-year-old son, helped take the beasts on down the glen to Bridge of Balgie. He too showed an unsuspected aptitude for the work. It was a question of pace as much as anything. Children, like cattle, are easily distracted, their curiosity browsing along the wayside. Evidently it pleased the beasts not to be the objects of relentless attention and they responded to the more staccato rhythm by straying little and invariably grazing their way forwards. Occasional bursts of erratic energy did not bother them. With the exception of Matilda, who was rarely pleased by anything, they seemed rather to enjoy the company and tastes of someone nearer their own age.

13

'Who would be a drover then?'

GLEN LYON TO CRIEFF

From Bridge of Balgie in Glen Lyon the drove struck up the flanks of Ben Lawers. It was the last hill but one. Although the only reasonable route followed the line of the minor road there was soft going on the grass verges. The descent to Loch Tay on the other side looked to be more difficult. Now forestry crowded the road; the boys would have to slither down two miles of steep tarmac to the loch and then, because of fences and hedges, follow the busy main road into Killin. I scouted ahead for a kinder cross-country route and then waited by the Ben Lawers Visitor Centre to head them off.

The lee of a stone dyke provided shelter from the wind and, to keep awake, I pulled out a letter that had been in my pocket for weeks. The address was particularly pleasing: *'John Keay, Drover, Taking Highland Cattle from Skye to Falkirk, Glenelg PO, Wester Ross'*. At the top it said 'Please Deliver'; the Glenelg PO had obliged. The letter inside was unsigned and the only clue to the sender was an Ullapool post mark. Having much to say but only a scrap of paper on which to say it the writer had been forced to cramp both his writing and his style. Additionally much of it was not in English. Without so much as a 'Dear Sir' it came straight to the point.

> The big event of your trip will be after you get to Falkirk [Crieff?] and you've sold the cattle. Then in keeping with old time tradition (as you couldn't get home that night anyway) you have a good going ceilidh – no women – a male ceilidh. No mushy love songs. No fishing or sailing songs. But droving songs, hunting songs, drinking songs etc. – a pastoral maybe. And poaching songs.

There followed several Gaelic titles – suggestions for the evening's programme – and then 'a real drover's song by a drover' which the writer kindly rendered in full. Obviously the original composer of this piece was not in the same class as Duncan Ban MacIntyre but, freely translated, it has a folkish and authentic flavour; it is no doubt typical of a host of similar popular airs.

The Song of the Drover

Morag of the tawny hair
Were she here we'd sing a song;
Glad I'd be to have her with me,
Never feel the journey long.

Young I was when first I went
O'er the hills and through the vales;
Twenty years and more I've spent
Droving cattle to the sales.

Morag of the tawny hair etc.

I've bought bullocks black and red
Known them by their ears and tails,
Many weary days I've had
On the long road to the sales.

Morag of the tawny hair etc.

Sometimes, when the drove was over,
Scarce the cows and cross the men.
Everyone would blame the drover;
Who would be a drover then?

Morag of the tawny hair etc.

The mysterious letter ended as abruptly as it had begun: 'well, your weather could be better but have a good ceilidh.' He was right about the weather but I was more intrigued by what he had to say about the end of the drove. In the closing stages the pressures mounted. 'Everyone would blame the drover; who would be a drover then?' In the old days, whether the destination was Crieff or Falkirk, the droves neared the tryst through a tightening net of restrictions and

exactions. Amongst the carefully walled fields and swards of
the Lowlands they were forced to follow roads already con-
gested with the traffic of other droves and of buyers. Every
bite of grass had to be paid for and the closer the tryst the
higher the charge. There were old friends to greet but there
were also thieves, creditors and pick-pockets. Unlike the
Highlanders in their remote glens, the good folk of Crieff were
none too pleased to welcome them. Although they would
complain bitterly when the trade moved to Falkirk, they had
no love for the uncouth drovers. 'Bare-footed and bare-
headed', according to a local schoolmaster, they were liable to
'enter the houses of the country people, take unceremonious
possession of their firesides and beds, carry off the potatoes
from their fields and gardens, and sometimes even the blankets that had afforded them a temporary covering for the night.'
The drovers responded by resenting these comfortable folk
almost as much as their grazing charges and market fees. It
was a time of acute anxiety; for over all hung the massive
uncertainty of a market which could abort the long weeks of
travel and make or break a man in a matter of minutes.

Dugald MacDougall, the Argyllshire drover, cherished an
apposite story told him by his grandfather. It concerned two
great-great-uncles who had had to face the drover's ultimate
dilemma. Having reached the tryst they discovered that the
best price they could hope for was less than that they had
guaranteed to the owners of the cattle back in Argyll. What to
do? Should they sell at a loss and throw themselves on the
mercies of the Argyllshire farmers? Or, having already gone
over the top, should they simply pocket the money and make
off?

Well, they considered. The one spoke to the other [what] was the
best thing they could do. And the other brother advised him and
he said, 'The only thing that I can do, that I think we ought to do,
and keep our own credit, and do the best we can for the people at
home, is take them back, everyone of these animals, to the owner
that had them when he sold them, and deliver them to the owner

at his own farm where we bought them, and tell them that that's
the best thing we can do. We can't pay the money that we ought to
pay; but there's your animals as we found them.' So they [the
farmers] had so much confidence in them after that they would
give them any cattle they wanted without paying for them; for
they could take them away to sell and pay them when they came
back.

The idea of having to retrace all those miles made me faintly
hysterical. And would they want Matilda back on South Uist?
Would von Simpson and the brindle twins settle down again
on fenceless Knoydart? Anyway, we had to sell; the bank
wanted its money back.

As a volley of hailstones rattled on the dyke the first beasts
breasted the brow of the hill. They looked more resolute than
ever. Heads down, forelocks windswept and horns gently
dipping, they were magnificent. But in the ring, and against
beasts that had been carefully prepared for the sale and then
whisked from their lush meadows to the market, what chance
did they stand? Between the drove's end at Crieff and the sale
at Stirling they would have less than a week. It would be time
enough for sore feet to recover but not for putting on any
weight. And there would be no hiding the fact that these were
the cattle that had walked from Skye. Their celebrity might
even command a premium; equally they might be marked
down as beasts that had had the flesh walked off them by a
bunch of publicity-seeking incompetents.

At the moment the publicity was paying dividends. Unlike
the drovers of old our passage was getting easier as we
approached Crieff. 'Ah, I wondered when you would be showing up,' said the lady of Morenish farm when we enquired
about a stance above Killin. In the pub that evening the drinks
were on the house and next day a sizeable crowd accompanied
the drove through the little town. At Crieff a formal reception
was in preparation. The children were to be given a day off
school, the press would be invited to a jamboree in the old
Mart Park, and the sponsors would get their last bite at the

publicity cake. Captain Coutts was master-minding the operation along with Famous Grouse Whisky. He had found a field for the night before the triumphal entry and he would graze the beasts free of charge at his own farm until the sale.

'Heavens, you look tired,' said Tricia from Famous Grouse as we met to agree the final arrangements. Tired? Oddly it had not occurred to me that either cattle or drovers might become exhausted. All along we had thought in terms of getting acclimatised, settling down, getting fitter. But now that she said it, and now that I came to look at the others, it was obvious. We were all knackered. For some days past every halt had been greeted by the cattle going down and the drovers quickly following them. Getting started again depended on someone making a conscious effort to stay awake or on George or Russell, both mighty snorers, sounding the alarm. With the change to drier, colder weather and gentler gradients a heavy lassitude had settled upon the party. Conversation slowed to a trickle. JP had long since given up on *Zen and the Art . . .* and the only reading in circulation was the Ordnance Survey. The last miles were slipping past in a daze of routine.

There had been a time when who did what had seemed a matter of moment. Unlike an expedition up the Amazon, there was nothing to ensure the cohesion of this little exercise. Anyone could push off whenever they wanted to. They could check into the nearest hotel and be on the bus home in the morning; most of us were self-employed with infinitely more profitable ways of spending our time. There was therefore never any question of ordering one another around. Everything depended on each person willingly doing his share of a workload which grew no lighter for being endlessly repetitive.

But somewhere north of Rannoch Moor, up by Blackwater perhaps, a pattern of existence had simply imposed itself. Gavin or George saw to the feeding and welfare of the beasts, Russell or Julia cooked supper and looked after the ponies, Chris did his rounds, JP pitched tents, I did breakfast. The electric fence went up and it came down; the footbath was filled, the beasts put through it, and the bath emptied; the ponies were fed, saddled and packed, then unpacked, unsaddled and fed again; Land Rover and trailer were repeatedly unloaded and reloaded; food was ordered and bought, feedstuffs and hay replenished. As the dramas diminished, routine ruled. Mentally as well as physically we had slowed to the pace of a zombie-like plod; even 'a drop of the cratur' produced only a short spurt of animation.

Looking back it becomes crystal clear. The boys had won. They had finally reduced their drovers to their own dogged pace. We no longer scampered about their flanks to let off energy; we had none and anyway it was unnecessary. You could dawdle along in the midst of the beasts and, unless there was some need to push them, they would stay with you. The bond of trust between beast and man was complete. But it was we who had compromised. As sponsors and well-wishers took charge of our final movements it was hard to resist the impression that we, the drovers, were now as much the driven as the cattle. Indeed the distinction between the two was being blurred. The drove had become an entity, men and cattle moving and thinking in a plodding harmony. 'They' were no longer the boys but the friends and well-wishers who were homing in on the final act. And if their demands conflicted with those of the boys there was no question where our sympathies lay. I doubt if 'they' understood this; even at this remove, to explain it without invoking sentiment I find almost impossible.

In *The Goshawk* T. H. White graphically describes the tussle involved in training a bird of prey. For days and nights he sits up with his hawk, fighting off sleep in a remorseless battle of wills which must end with the bird eventually succumbing to its new master. Cattle droving, I had once imagined, might entail something of the same struggle for mastery. In fact it turned out to be the complete opposite. There had been no epic battle, just a steady and imperceptible erosion of all notions of contest and authority. The beasts had not

15 Down from the hills. Cattle and drovers pass through Comrie with five miles to journey's end

16 Matilda, wayward Hebridean matron, in retirement amongst the daffodils of Loch Awe-side. With her is the calf she carried from Skye

really 'won'. We had all simply learnt to live, to move and to think together. That bond between drover and beasts had more to do with experience than sentiment. The consensus of the herd now included each individual drover as well as each individual beast. This sense of communion, plus the slower pace, hinted at an alternative source of strength, a less erratic and assertive way of living, a more receptive outlook.

I know this sounds pretentious; it is indeed the result of rationalising after the event. At the time I was aware only of being very tired yet highly elated. The three remaining days were some of the longest and most exhausting of the whole journey. We moved in a heady trance which even the odd drama failed to break. Nothing, it seemed, could get through to us. There was a soft singing within; such an overwhelming sense of fulfilment had to be more than mere self-satisfaction at having made it to the end of the trail.

From Killin, which Dorothy Wordsworth neatly characterised as a place at variance with itself, 'the ordinary half-village, half-town bustle of an everyday place' being belied by 'the extreme natural wildness' of the Dochart river which crashes alongside the main street in a series of cataracts – from this half-Highland, half-Lowland place, gale number fifteen bore the drove up into the hills on the south side of Loch Tay. The gale was authentically Highland, indeed Hebridean. Near Loch Breachclaich we found a natural hollow hemmed in by rock which was just big enough to take the cattle. There was no shelter for the drovers and early next morning the big green mess tent finally succumbed to the blast. The ridge pole, all of two and a half inches in diameter, simply snapped like a twig. JP had always ridiculed this tent as thoroughly unprofessional. He said it belonged in a boy scout camp and that it offended his sense of what was proper on a serious expedition. Too often he had had to pitch it single-handed. But the tent had the last word, souring his moment of triumph by collapsing when our brownie was within busy with the washing-up.

On November 4th the destination was Glen Lednock. In the

old days all this high ground between Loch Tay and Strathearn must have been alive with droves. At Killin cattle from Glen Lyon and Rannoch Moor were joined by droves from Argyll and Mull as well as those from Skye, Morvern and Ardnamurchan who had crossed the watershed at Tyndrum. Whether they headed straight into the hills – as did we – or whether they held to the lochside as far as Ardeonaig, all now surged in a continuous flow towards Glen Lednock. Thence a day's journey would take them down into Strathearn and, via Comrie, into Crieff.

They did not, however, have to contend with 'Loch Lednock'. After ten joyous hours of meandering over the hillside, savouring the last day of upland freedom, we dropped down to the edge of this ugly and artificial reservoir; before the glen was dammed there was not even a lochan here. Now the water had obliterated all sign of human habitation. Instead of the fields, the paths and the cottages of this once fertile hollow there was just a steely sheet of water fringed by bleached chunks of rock and trapped beneath steep slopes covered with an impenetrable tangle of waist-high heather. An evil track of loose chips alternating with gritty tarmac offered the only way ahead. By seven o'clock we were limping, stumbling and shouting in pitch darkness.

'How many have you got?'

'God knows. Maybe ten I think. Hang on. There are more up above.'

'Is Matilda there?'

'Don't think so. Must be with George.'

'George.' No answer. 'Where the hell is he?'

'Sat down, I think. Must have fallen asleep.'

'OK, that's it. Let's stop where we are. Otherwise we'll all get lost.'

An icy breeze blew off the loch but deep in the heather it was deliciously, soporifically, sheltered. A hush as impenetrable as the darkness settled over all. Occasionally a beast coughed. Growing accustomed to the silence, I picked out the snort that accompanies George's snoring rhythm. He was some way off but unlikely to go any further.

Half an hour later the lights of the Land Rover appeared above us. It was lucky we had stopped; evidently the track doubled back over the ridge. The rescue party brought hot soup and torches. They said it was still two or three miles to the stance. With the utmost reluctance men and cattle picked themselves out of the heather and stumbled on. Both were so dozy that at the first cattle grid four of the boys simply tottered straight in. Too weary to panic they extricated themselves without harm. At ten o'clock we finally reached the tents; we had been on the go for fifteen hours. And there were yet the usual chores – beasts to be fed and watered, food to be cooked and eaten, drams to be drunk against another icy night.

Next morning the boys were fed at first light and, while we breakfasted, they simply filed out of their field. As if responding to some inexorable homing instinct, they strolled off down the glen, swung right, away from the road up to the dam, and held their course straight for Comrie. When we finally caught up with them Matilda threw us a 'what kept you?' scowl and kept on going. It can only have been coincidence that the one morning on which they took matters into their own hands happened to be the last. All that day they behaved so impeccably that to the people who lined the streets of Comrie it must have seemed that droving was absurdly easy. Not a single front garden was violated, not a car nudged, not a toddler terrified. On the corner of the High Street three butchers in striped aprons and with their arms folded across their chests stood on the kerb and knowingly appraised each haunch and rib cage. The boys peered sweetly back, gazing shyly through silken forelocks.

The very weather rose to the occasion and Strathearn, a vale rather than a glen, basked in continuous sunshine. Ennobled by what Dorothy Wordsworth called 'many gentlemen's seats under the hills', the fields and woods had a park-like feel.

Pheasants honked from behind the hedges and well-bred mares ridden by well-bred ladies in riding hats clip-clopped along the roadside. Mhari, Eilidh and Rona, their manes and tails long and shaggy and their panniers and packsaddles tattered and battered, suddenly looked like gipsy waifs.

In an adjacent field a herd of tubby Aberdeen-Angus came gallumphing down to the roadside. They pressed cheeky noses through the fence and for a moment our boys were roused from their torpor. Clambering up the bank they raised their monumental heads to rub noses with the sleek black strangers. Compared to the hairy splendour of the Highlanders the locals looked obscenely naked. They wobbled and quivered all over and their eyes started out of their sockets. They were comfy little clerks, all short backs and sides with obtrusive ears and polished chaps. It was a meeting of two irreconcilable worlds, the wild and the tame, the natural and the man-made. Here, across a barbed-wire fence, was the difference between a hydro reservoir and a Highland loch, between a block of sitka spruce and an upland spinney of birch and rowan, between a slashed and blasted access track and a hill path. And perhaps between the stress of trucking cattle and the wonderful absurdity of droving them.

About a mile short of Crieff we turned off into a field. Across the strath the town's grey terraced streets could be seen spilling down the hillside, eddying round a church spire and ducking a concrete supermarket. The lights were coming on. Smoke from a thousand coal grates rose in the still air to merge with chilly fronds of fog that crept in on the evening. With the sun had gone the autumn. The hedgerows here were threadbare and a couple of ash trees with not a leaf between them stood braced for the winter. We counted the cattle into the field; they made straight for the trailer in expectation of supper. Then we closed the gate. It was the end of the road.

As if to excel the hospitality of all previous stances, Peter Halley, the owner of the field, also made his home ours. One of the baths was circular, sunken and big enough for a family.

The hot water gushed from the faucet like a geyser. We emerged in turn, scrubbed, brushed and born again, radiating a glow of well-being. Never have shoes felt so light nor sofas so sumptuous. In the drawing-room firelight danced on polished glass and parquet flooring. Even the whisky tasted finer from hefty crystal tumblers. Paradise is antithesis. In the glare of the desert, Arab warriors dreamt of shaded gardens with tinkling streams and languid maidens; the Highland drover would happily have settled for the comforts of Lochlane House.

Next day, at the civilised hour of 10.30 a.m., we formed up on the outskirts of the town. If anyone doubted that the drovers were now the driven it was borne out by the order of march: police escort first, then the pipers, then the press and television, then the dogs, the thirty head of cattle, the drovers, the SPCA, the ponies, and finally more police. Uncertain how the boys would react to the bagpipes, the only concession we asked was that the pipers should keep a respectable distance. 'Pipers miffed', reported JP.

Crowds lined the pavements and trooped along behind. Some clapped as we passed; it seemed inappropriate. A small girl with pigtails tendered the Monarch her packet of crisps and a young matador tried to interest Matilda in his red scarf. Neither cattle nor drovers paid much attention. As we wheeled into the playing fields, once the old mart, to a shaking of hands and a drinking of drams, 'they' had us firmly under control. Julia and the ponies, Gavin and the dogs, George and Matilda, JP and Chris and von Simpson and the Brindles, the big beasts and the small – we were all being paraded. We were in the ring; we were under the hammer.

★   ★   ★

There are no accounts of how the Crieff tryst was organised or what the scene may have looked like. By the 1770s when Dr Johnson and Thomas Pennant made their pioneering journeys in the Highlands, the bulk of the trade was already going to Falkirk. Although only twenty-five miles south of Crieff,

Falkirk lies in the central belt of Scotland just next to Edinburgh with its good communications to England. As English
buyers increasingly dominated the trade it was inevitable that
the market most convenient for them would see the best
prices. Pennant says 24,000 beasts were sold there in 1772
while another writer of the period puts the number for the
October tryst at up to 50,000 with perhaps as many again
being sold at the smaller sales in August and September.

'I have a vision', wrote the Rev. Norman MacLeod, 'of
miles of tents, of flocks and herds, surpassed only by those in
the wilderness of Sinai; of armies of Highland sellers trying to
get high prices out of Englishmen and Englishmen trying to
put off the Highlandmen with low prices – but all in the way of
fair dealing.' MacLeod, the man who was once Queen Victoria's
chaplain and latterly a minister on Skye, never actually
attended the tryst. But to even the remotest Highland parish
so crucial was its conduct – 'on it the rent and income of the
year depended' – that it was impossible not to be well informed as to its every detail.

> When any person returned who had been himself at the market,
> who could recount its ups and downs, its sales and purchases, with
> all the skirmishes, stern encounters and great victories, it was a
> great day . . . There was such enjoyment in details, such a luxury
> in going over all the prices, and all that was asked by the seller and
> refused by the buyer, and asked again by the buyer and refused
> again by the seller, with such nice financial fencing of 'splitting
> the difference' or giving back a 'luck-penny', as baffles all descrip-
> tion. It was not enough to give the prices of three year olds and
> four year olds, yell cows, crock ewes, stirks, stots, lambs, tups,
> wethers, shots, bulls etc. but the stock of each well known prop-
> rietor or breeder had to be discussed. Colonsay's bulls, Cor-
> riechoillie's sheep, Drumdriesaig's heifers, or Achadashenaig's
> wethers had all to be passed under careful review. Then followed
> discussions about 'distinguished beasts' which had fetched high
> prices, their horns, their hair, their houghs, and general 'fashion',
> with their parentage . . . And after all was gone over it was a
> pleasure to begin the same tune again with variations.

By the mid-nineteenth century the number of beasts sold

annually at Falkirk had risen to its climax of nearly 150,000 with at least 100,000 sheep. Such a concourse covered the ground for many miles in every direction and went on for several days. The 200 fenced acres where the actual selling took place was just the focus of 'a scene to which certainly Great Britain, possibly the whole world, does not offer a parallel'. 'All,' continued Thomas Gisborne in 1849, 'is animation, bustle, business and activity; servants running about, shouting to the cattle, keeping them together in their particular lots, and ever and anon cudgels are at work upon the horns and rumps of the restless animals that attempt to wander in search of grass or water.'

Around the ground there sprang up a small and temporary town. Four or five wooden huts announced themselves as banks, 'The Royal Bank of Scotland', 'The Commercial Bank', 'The British Linen Company'. Here the English dealer tied his horse and disappeared inside to draw the cash for his purchases. The money changed hands in a separate booth and as often as not was being redeposited by a Highland drover in a matter of minutes. It was unwise to enter the mêlée outside with a pocket full of notes. Besides all manner of sideshows, sixty or seventy tents sold just food and liquor. The cooking was on open fires under an awning with vats of broth much in evidence. Inside dealers and drovers vied with pedlars, jugglers, gamblers, fruit sellers, ballad singers and beggars. 'What an indescribable clamour prevails in most of these parti-coloured abodes,' wrote Gisborne.

> Far into the afternoon, when frequent calls have elevated the spirits and stimulated the colloquial powers of the visitors, a person hears the uncouth Cumberland jargon and the prevailing Gaelic, along with innumerable provincial dialects, in their genuine purity, mingled in one astounding roar. All seem inclined to speak; and raising their voices to command attention, the whole of the orators are obliged to bellow as loudly as they can possibly roar.

There was no auctioneer and no regular system of bidding.

Buyers rode on horseback amongst the herds and, after 'a good deal of riggling', simply agreed a price with the head drover. The buyer then 'claps a penny of arles in the hand of the stockholder, observing at the same time "It's a bargain". Tar dishes are then got and the purchasers mark being put upon the cattle, they are driven from the field.' Presumably the temptation to hang on indefinitely in expectation of a higher price was offset by tryst charges mounting the longer the beasts were on the ground.

In the second half of the nineteenth century numbers attending the market dropped dramatically and by the 1890s there would seem to have been room on the main ground for all. Dugald MacDougall, the Argyllshire drover, remembered taking as much care to sort and show his beasts to advantage as does a seller in the auction ring today. Each lot was closely bunched and driven round in a circle. 'And the buyer was standing on the outside and he was seeing them all as they were coming round. And if possible, if there was one that wasn't so good, it was to try to keep that one in the middle; let the rest keep him out of sight. The buyer saw them all but they were all on the inside.'

Like many drovers MacDougall had his regular customers; for instance 'a Mr Carr from Yorkshire' always bought any heifers he had. Each drover, like each breeder, had his reputation for a certain class of cattle and often droves were spoken for before they even materialised. Such informal business connections must greatly have speeded up the tryst. But as local markets at the extremities of the new railway lines – at Aberdeen, Inverness and Oban – usurped the pre-eminence of Falkirk, such arrangements foundered and the role of the drover as liaison between breeder and fattener was taken over by the auctioneer.

Today the greater flexibility offered by road transport again favours centralisation. At Kildean outside Stirling, and almost half-way between Crieff and Falkirk, United Auctions (Scotland) operate what is claimed to be the biggest livestock mart in Europe. Like Falkirk the site is dictated by communications. The acres of pens are hard by the last exit on the M9 motorway. It is in effect the roadhead of the British motorway system. From here south, high-speed juggernauts can average seventy miles per hour all the way to London; but north the roads are twisty and steep, more suited to the battered transporters of Highland contractors.

With its bars and restaurants and banks, and with numerous sales in simultaneous progress in different rings, Kildean is not unlike Falkirk. It may look a bit like a railway terminus but in the concourse and the beer halls the conversation is just as animated, the vocabulary just as baffling. 'Ring 3, Alley S and T, at 1.00 p.m. – Sale of Highland Drove Cattle' announced the catalogue in a display entry. We were to follow a Mr Aitken's eight Friesian bullocks and to be followed by the only other Highlanders on the programme which were entered by Captain Coutts and our old friend Hughie MacDonald of Oban. This was surely a coincidence; it could only be a good sign that both men thought that there might be a demand worth cashing in on.

In the five days of rest and recuperation between Crieff and the sale we had seen the boys only once. Now, in the pens, we polished their horns with linseed oil and tidied and brushed their coats. There was no sense of estrangement. As Julia snipped at the mats in Ickle Brindle's body valance he looked as if he might roll over to have his tummy rubbed. George was bubbling with pride. Instead of losing weight the boys had actually gained a few kilos since their weigh-in before the drove at Oban.

'Beasts is looking great,' he kept saying. 'Now we'll see, John. Ach yes, just great.'

I was, as usual, less confident. There was a crowd round the pens and it was said that the ring was so packed that people were being turned away. But they might all be there just out of curiosity; nothing pulls a crowd like publicity. What I could not work out was what sort of price we needed to avoid financial embarrassment. It had to be something like the £300 per beast that we had paid. Would £320 do? It might; but no one was going to pay that much for the smaller beasts. It had to be at least £350 for the big ones. No, more.

With a crashing of steel gates, alleys S and T opened and we surged out of the pens. A young stockman yelled down the line 'Here come the Highlanders' and his colleagues hastily vaulted out of the way. 'Christ, look at the horns,' muttered another. They gaped with amazement as Gavin patted a dawdler and George threw a final arm round Matilda.

In the ring Jimmy Weir, the chief auctioneer, said a few inspiriting words. I followed with a short tribute to the boys, and the sale began. The first pair, neither the best nor the worst, fetched £480 each; the Brindles, von Simpson and the Monarch went for £500 apiece; even Ickle Brindle got £250. They were the highest prices on record for beasts of their class.

As the boys trooped through in twos and threes, each group accompanied by one of the drovers, it became like a passing out parade. The great agricultural machine had thrown up these thirty beasts at random. They had been ours for a couple of months. During that time they had become famous as a group and beloved as individuals. Now they were being sucked back into the anonymous machine. I felt like one of those big game conservationists who, when the time comes, must release back into the wild some briefly cherished but always borrowed creature.

Only Matilda was to feature any more in our lives. She was bought by Russell and on the shores of Loch Awe she settled to a life of ease. Her coat grew thicker, her gait more graceful. She blossomed into matronly magnificence and in the spring she gave birth to the calf that she had carried all the way from Skye.

Bibliography

Aitken, R. *The West Highland Way,* 1980.

Alexander, W. *Notes and Sketches Illustrative of Northern Rural Life in the Eighteenth Century,* 1877.

Anon. *Sketch of a Tour in the Highlands in Sept and Oct 1818,* 1819.

Bonser, K. J. *The Drovers,* 1970.

Boswell, J. *The Journal of a Tour in the Hebrides with S. Johnson,* 1813 edn.

Burt, E. *Letters from a Gentleman in the North of Scotland,* 1815 edn.

Cameron, A. *The Lochaber Drover, Corriechoillie,* n.d.

Cregeen, E. 'Recollections of an Argyllshire Drover' in *Scottish Studies* 3, 1959.

Cumming, C. E. G. *In the Hebrides,* 1883.

Darling, F. Fraser *West Highland Survey,* 1955.

Dixon, H. H. *Field and Fern or Scottish Flocks and Herds,* 1865.

Gisborne, T. *Essays on Agriculture,* 1854.

Grant, A. *Letters from the Mountains 1773–1803,* 1806.

Haldane, A. R. B. *The Drove Roads of Scotland,* 1952.

Highland Cattle Society *The Highland Herd Book; Retrospective Volume,* 1885.

—— *Highland Breeders' Journal,* 1980, 1981, 1982.

Housman, W. *Cattle Breeds and Management,* 1897.

Hunter, J. *The Making of the Crofting Community,* 1976.

Johnson, S. *A Journey to the Western Isles of Scotland,* 1816 edn.

McCombie, W. *Cattle and Cattle Breeders,* 1886.

MacCulloch, J. *The Highlands and Western Isles of Scotland,* 1824.

Mackie, J. D. *A History of Scotland*, 1964.

MacLean, G. R. D. *Poems of the Western Highlands*, 1961.

MacLean, M. *The Literature of the Highlands*, 1904.

MacLeod, A. (ed.) *The Songs of Duncan Ban MacIntyre*, 1952.

MacLeod, N. *Reminiscences of a Highland Parish*, 1867.

Martin, M. *A Description of the Western Isles of Scotland in c.1695*, 1703.

Mitchell, J. *Reminiscences of My Life in the Highlands*, 1883.

Murray, W. H. *The Scottish Highlands*, 1976.

Nimmo, W. *History of Stirlingshire*, 1777.

Palmer, W. T. *The Verge of the Scottish Highlands*, 1947.

Pennant, T. *A Tour in Scotland and Voyage to the Hebrides*, 1774.

Pennell, J. and E. R. *Our Journey to the Hebrides*, 1890.

Porteous, A. *History of Crieff*, 1912.

Prebble, J. *The Highland Clearances*, 1963.

Robertson, J. *General View of the Agriculture in the County of Inverness*, 1808.

Scott, W. *Rob Roy*, 1901 edn.

——, *Two Drovers*, 1901 edn.

Sinclair, C. *Scotland and the Scotch or The Western Circuit*, 1840.

Smith, A. *A Summer in Skye*, 1866.

Southey, R. *Journal of a Tour in Scotland in 1819*, 1929 edn.

Taylor, W. *The Military Roads of Scotland*, 1976.

Wordsworth, D. *Recollections of a Tour made in Scotland in 1803*, 1874 edn.

Youatt, W. *Cattle, their Breeds, Management, Diseases*, 1889.

Youngson, A. J. (ed.) *Beyond the Highland Line*, 1974.